HOW TO BECOME AN
ANGEL

Rudolf Joseph Lorenz Steiner
February 27, 1861 – March 30, 1925

FROM THE WORKS OF DR. RUDOLF STEINER

HOW TO BECOME AN
ANGEL

PREPARING FOR THE FUTURE
SIXTH & SEVENTH EPOCHS

Dr. Douglas J. Gabriel

Our Spirit, LLC
2023

OUR SPIRIT, LLC

P. O. Box 355
Northville, MI 48167

www.ourspirit.com
www.neoanthroposophy.com
www.gospelofsophia.com
www.eternalcurriculum.com

2023 Copyright © by Our Spirit, LLC

ISBN: 979-8-9864415-3-5 (paperback)
ISBN: 979-8-9864415-4-2 (eBook)

CONTENTS

How to Become
an Angel

What are you evolving towards? Perhaps an Angel, freed from the confines of the prison-like suffering of the world, or perhaps the opposite—a devolved sub-human cyborg that sinks back into animality with mechanical thinking, cold-hearted feelings, and atrophied willpower that has been given over to machines and robots that do our thinking, feeling, and willing for us. Everything we give over to mechanical machines to accomplish for us diminishes human capacities and hinders the evolution of those capacities into higher forms of thinking, feeling, and willing—becoming an Angel. Do you know which direction you are going? Are you going forward or backward, up or down? Generally, most people do not think about such troublesome thoughts because it might cause them to realize that they have no workable cosmology that informs them about how humans got here and where they are going.

A good secular humanist might quickly answer the question by saying that they "believe" in science and the dangerous and unimaginative future that mad-scientists are creating in their laboratories at this moment. Every heinous depredation of the human body, soul, and spirit is on the agenda of godless scientist—the high priests of the religion of the "scientific method." But unfortunately, scientists have little imagination, creativity, or morality to aim at humanity's future with faith, hope, or love. Science theories are simply the newest bad idea of a tinkering, greedy scientist who lacks a comprehensive cosmology. These money worshiping demagogues try to force-feed humanity a materialistic cosmology wherein the entire universe was created from a small ball of matter the size of a golf ball that exploded into the organized galaxies of the Cosmos. Any sane person should discount anything else that a person who "believes" this nonsense doctrine, via "faith" in science, says afterwards. There is no viable scientific explanation for creation, ectropy, life, or what they call "intelligent design." Science worships destruction, entropy, death and it denies that "consciousness" or "beings" might be behind intelligent design.

Science is a new type of religion that requires faith in scientists, but godless scientists lead this anti-religion with ever-changing theories that are half-truths at best. Religion should provide us with a worldview relinking us with the original source of all things; while materialistic science defines us as insignificant grains of sand on an endless, meaningless beach. For materialistic science denies the original source of all things due to a lack of morality in the realms of imagination, inspiration, and intuition. Rudolf Steiner clearly indicates that the imaginative language of the ancient myths and religions give us much better ideas of the beings behind the workings of nature. While materialistic scientists relentlessly deny the invisible sources at the core of burgeoning life; when in fact, they can only partially understand certain death processes. In keeping with this, there are no comprehensive scientific theories for the sources of life: warmth, fire, light, wisdom, sound, life, ectropy, levity, growth, living morphology, evolutionary goals, human metamorphoses, or any other truly critical aspect of life. Materialistic science simply denies morality, grace, love, goodness, beauty, truth, or any other virtue that emanates from the divine beings behind intelligent design. Scientists call that nihilistic perspective "objective." We cannot look to modern science for a realistic cosmology.

Science, art, and religion should be combined into applicable ideas that provide a realistic cosmology answering the many questions that modern materialistic science ignores. The most expensive science endeavors in history have been the ridiculously foolish cyclotrons that have attempted to blow up matter with accelerated particles trying to prove that the "Big Bang Theory" is true. This is, of course, compounded stupidity. It is well-known that the observer of phenomena changes that which is observed as matter vacillates between the particle and wave state via the observer's perception. Thus, scientists see what they "want" to see, not what is actually manifesting in phenomena as reality. Everything in theoretical science is simply the opinion of sense-bound, godless mad-scientists that will sooner or later be disproven and supplanted by another opinion. These scientists and inventors are seemingly unmonitored and unchecked by anyone for the immoral and harmful consequences of their "innovations." We live in a scientifically controlled world of changing theories that do more harm than good. Scientific "advancements" are often never analyzed for the inherent harm they can do to innocent human beings that ultimately add to the devolution of humanity. There is no "settled science" due to a lack of a comprehensive cosmology that works. In today's world, when you "follow the science", it leads you to the worship of money and the funding of corporate research for weapons of death, both military and pharmaceutical.

Where do you personally get your idea of the future that describes what you are ultimately evolving towards? If you have religious beliefs, you might be moving towards the inspirations of those who originated and developed a belief system (cosmology) found in one or another religion. But did you yourself have a direct revelation of those religious ideas? Did you experience what the creators of your religion preached, or do you believe this cosmology through faith? Oftentimes, people inherit the cosmology of their parents, family members, or friends without once asking if it is true, applicable, or a reality they can personally experience. They accept it based on the apparent faith of others.

A modern person may not be able to formulate a single question about the nature of creation, God, or spiritual realms because they have become lazy and let the priest or guru do their thinking for them. The same is true of modern materialists and their sacred scientism. Most people do not have a clue about what electricity is or how gravity works, or even how their computers and machines work. They leave that heavy thinking to the scientists. The common person lives their life in subservience to invisible scientists and inventors who control life in general, and their personal life in particular. "My doctor told me to take this medicine; therefore, the side-effects are not my fault. I didn't read the insert that told me the drug could kill me, and the doctor never told me anything about side-effects," might be the last words of a good believer in science who is dying from iatrogenic death – death via a doctor, who is a "good scientist" who "believes in science." The materialist's scientific belief system doesn't work very well because it usurps the free will of the human being, thus hindering their spiritual evolution and promoting devolution. We must "wake up" to evolve, but materialists prefer the sleepy world of godless scientism where the dream-theories of scientists lull us into dark devolution.

When I look at a person in the capacity of a teacher, I am looking for the Angel inside of them that will blossom in the future. I don't hold a partial view of who they appear to be now, limited by their inherited characteristics, family beliefs, scientific misunderstandings, or their developing capacities. I look beyond nature and nurture to what their spirit has developed as higher aspirations, hopes, and ideals. These moral and spiritual qualities can pull a person up from any limitations of birth, social circumstance, or limited religious beliefs. Revelations and inspiration are available to anyone who rises above their circumstances and reaches for divine virtues instead of wallowing in Earthly vices. Heavenly virtues lead beyond the present human condition into the Divine Plan where humans emulate the beings of creation who gave us life and love and designed us "in their image." Once the cosmological vision of what a human can become is held firmly in the heart, humans may then evolve beyond the animal-human and human kingdoms into the realm of Angel-humans and Angels.

One problem with evolving into an Angel is that the human mind, deluded by the illusion that sense perceptible matter is all that there is to life, can pull the soul of a human backward in evolution to the animalistic path of the Seven Deadly Sins— the dark vices that kill, instead of the heavenly virtues that give life. Every thought, feeling, or deed either creates the wings of our evolving Angel-hood or the horns of our devolving animalhood. Every virtuous human deed directs the effects to a light-filled future, whereas the selfish effects of vices are directed towards a dark future in opposition to the Divine Plan. If you haven't decided which one you are aiming at, then you are probably devolving towards a sub-natural world of darkness instead of a super-natural world of wisdom-filled light. Even the lukewarm attitude of an agnostic is drawing the soul and spirit into dark realms because they are not keeping up with progressive spiritual evolution. Actually, standing still is ultimately going backwards in evolution. Leaving your spiritual work to the priest or simply going to church to sing and pray may not be developing your personal understanding of how to become an Angel.

If you imagine an Angel with wings, a halo, no feet, dressed in a white tunic, playing a heavenly instrument, singing praises inside of a heavenly choir or mansion, then you are incorrect. Concepts of Angels derived from the materialistic, sense-bound world do not apply to non-material beings. If you want to imagine an Angel, you will need to pray, meditate, and contemplate sense-free qualities and ideas, such as: grace, mercy, divinity, love, goodness, truth, beauty, and the many other virtues that weave through our material world and within our soul and spirt. Virtues invisibly stand behind human thought, feelings, and deeds. These virtues can be perceived with super-sensible organs that need to be developed through continuous practice. To evolve, we need to "perceive" the invisible beings and forces that manifest the physical world so that super-sensible organs of perception can evolve into the spiritual organs we need to perceive and communicate with Angels, Archangels, Archai, and other spiritual beings. Founders of traditional religions directly communicated with the spiritual hierarchy and the divine. They developed their super-sensible organs so that the language of the spirit became the language of spiritual development and religion—the language of Angels. Each person on the spiritual path moving towards their own Angel-hood needs to learn the virtuous language of the spirit.

In the past, some legendary heroes of religion and myth earned the power to understand the language of animals, birds, minerals, and plants. These "seers" were able to perceive what lives behind the visible world where invisible beings create the kingdoms of nature. This invisible world is where beings and forces actively create the sense perceptible world through a language of the spirit that is often called the "word", or the "logos", or the "life ether." This language of the spirit can be learned through study, prayer, meditation, and by directly experiencing super-sensible perception. The seer can look through matter to the spirit behind it. When this type of super-sensible perception happens, minerals, plants, and animals begin to reveal their true nature to the awakened perception of an Angel-human through the language of the spirit. We don't have to wait for death to find out if our priest or guru was right about the invisible realms. We can gain our "Angel wings" right now if we find the wisdom that a comprehensive cosmology can provide. If we know where we stand currently, and where we are headed, then the path up the mountain of spiritual development becomes clearer.

Unfortunately, many Westerners have lost touch with any source of cosmology and people flounder in their efforts to understand who they are, where they came from, and where they are going. We are a lost people wandering in the desert, looking for water without a map or the intuition to know where to find life and nourishment. We have been brain-washed by secular humanism and materialistic science to believe we came from an illogical and unbelievable "big bang" and are now dying through the forces of entropy, like a machine winding down to a cold, lifeless, dark grave with no hopes of an after-life. Materialistic scientific cosmologies lead to depression, despair, and soul-death. If there is no meaning, spirit, or life in a person's cosmology, then there is no reason to live a life that leads to a dead-end.

There are a few cosmologies available to the seeking soul, but very few comprehensive cosmologies that can be applied in real life. Ancient Hindu, Persian, Egyptian, and Greek cosmologies attempt to be comprehensive but are not very effective when applied in the current world. Belief in ancient divine beings requires faith on the part of the believer. That is why ancient philosophers and alchemists tried to understand the physical world as a manifestation of the spiritual world. Relinking the physical to the spiritual is the mission of religion and spiritual development, but the true test of these cosmologies is whether they can inform the aspirant by connecting them to living spiritual beings through a spiritual language that can communicate in both directions. We can pray to the divine, but what answer does the divine give us? We need to develop the "eyes that can see" and "ears that can hear" the spiritual world and its inhabitants so that a two-way communication can take place. We need to become our own personal and singular religion that relinks with our original source of being and the spiritual hierarchy that has selflessly donated our mineral, plant, and animal worlds as a home upon which humans can learn to communicate with the invisible creators of our world. If this language of the spirit is learned well, humans can become Angels through its use. We will be taught what the future holds by the Angels and hierarchies who are not bound by the limitations of space and time. We can be "birthed" into the childhood of our "Angel nature" and learn to "stand upright, speak, and think" like an Angel in the spiritual realm of the Angels where our true Spirit-Self resides. When this happens, we become free of the suffering and limitations of the physical material world and take wing into the Angel realms, no longer to be pulled backwards into sub-natural realms of darkness and deathly vices.

Dr. Rudolf Steiner presents in his works the clearest and most comprehensive cosmology of the universe and humanity that can be found. His purview includes the wisdom of the ancients and his own clairvoyant perception of the spiritual world and its manifestation in the physical realm. His predictions of future events have come true repeatedly and his teachings show us the path to becoming an Angel. He also tells us exactly what will happen if we choose to devolve—consciously or unconsciously. The past and the future are spelled out in amazing detail for those who are willing to study and work to understand Steiner's Spiritual Science. The cosmology, called Anthroposophy, proves its veracity through clearly describing the beings and forces that have created our past, are sustaining our life in the present, and will create the future with our help as co-creators.

To understand the future, we need to first become familiar with the iterations of the forms of life from the distant past that have laid down the foundations of our present kingdoms of nature on Earth. The Earth we know has gone through three past "incarnations" before this current incarnation of Earth. There is also a stage of development in between each incarnation of the Earth wherein the substance that is donated by the sacrifice of higher hierarchical beings dissolves and subsequently reorganizes in the next incarnation as a higher version of the previous metamorphosed kingdom. In this fashion, minerals, plants, and animals all perfected their nature in the three prior incarnations of the Earth. As each new kingdom was created, adding to the previous kingdoms, a new dimension was created simultaneously. Each new incarnation built on the previous sacrifices, donations, and gifts of the gods. Steiner called these prior kingdoms the "three elementary kingdoms of The Mothers." As humans on Earth, we are now building a new kingdom on top of the three previous ones with the help of the spiritual hierarchy. The three elementary kingdoms of The Mothers are coincident with the three kingdoms of nature and the three dimensions of space. Through the gifts of Christ and the Elohim, humans are currently adding a fourth kingdom, as well as the ability to create a fifth and sixth kingdom in the future.

Every human being has three bodies created during the three prior incarnations of the Earth – the physical, etheric, and astral bodies. We have a mineral-human, plant-human, and animal-human inside the soul and spirit of each human being. These are gifts from spiritual beings who have been "frozen", "enchanted", or "suspended" in space and time for a specific duration of time to accomplish the grand design of the evolving human spirit. As humans use the spiritual tool of consciousness, they can move through time and cancel space. The third dimension of space (3D) is dissolved when timelessness is attained through super-sensible perception. Consciousness is not bound by time because both the past and the future can be perceived when consciousness traverses the threshold between the physical and spiritual worlds and enters the Angelic realm of timelessness. This dissolution of 3D space through timelessness helps create the possibility for moral imaginations – spiritual thinking. Humans can also dissolve 2D space through becoming a being who can super-sensibly perceive the spaceless through moral inspirations – spiritual feeling. Likewise, 1D space can be dissolved through selflessly surrendering human consciousness itself through moral intuition – spiritual deeds. Ultimately, the human being is a 6D being after it evolves through the next three incarnations of the Earth.

Humans can move beyond 3D, 4D, and 5D space and live in 6D space by evolving through the ranks of the Angels, Archangels, and Archai and selflessly extinguishing what we currently understand about personal self-consciousness. When humans reach 6D existence, it will be the highest level of the hierarchy a human can become during this current great cycle of seven Earth incarnations – an Archai. In other words, human beings were created to become masters of their own spiritual trinity—moral imagination, moral inspiration, and moral intuition—and in so doing, evolve into Angels, Archangels, and Archai during the great cycle of Earth incarnations. This is the cosmological Divine Plan, to "make humanity in our own image." We are human seeds planted by eternal gods that are growing into Angels, but currently we can't see the overall process because time, space, and consciousness limit our perception of what is spiritually going on in the world around us. When we mature, we will be able to understand, create, and direct the evolution of our own body, soul, and spirit.

Dr. Steiner gives us the most complete set pieces to the puzzle of the cosmogenesis and anthropogenesis of the universe and humanity. His prolific characterizations of these beings and forces constitute a new "religion" or "relinking" that is directed by the aspirant defining their own path towards this wisdom, which Steiner calls the being "Anthroposophia", who is inspired by the hierarchical rank of spiritual beings called the Kyriotetes – the Spirits of Wisdom. Steiner tells us that the being of Anthroposophia inspired him with the wisdom of Spiritual Science and She is always ready to help every aspirant take the next step up the spiritual mountain using the cosmology he developed as a map for the journey.

Each stage of the journey is frightening if you can't see the trail of the past and the road to the future. The past bogs us down in anger and the future freezes us with fear, but a comprehensive picture of the topology of the ascent to the summit can give us the courage to go on towards the goal. We need to study the history of the evolution of humanity to understand how we got to where we are, so that we can build upon the highest qualities of the progressive development of humanity and claim our inheritance of living wisdom and love. We can analyze the ever-changing nature of the human being throughout history and project the future metamorphosis of the human soul as it grows into its spiritual self.

The study of cosmology is not easy and not for the weak-minded. One must be able to hold thoughts that are almost incomprehensible in the mind and then move through time to see how one dimension is built upon the previous. The aspirant of cosmology needs to separate out previous incarnations of the Earth and understand their specific metamorphosis while also being able to see their manifestation in our current Earth incarnation. This is called heterochrony. Seeing different times and substances (space) manifesting in the present as an accumulation of hierarchical and elemental beings is a first step in growing new super-sensible organs of perception that are not limited by space and time. When you defy or dissolve time, subsequently the 3D world will have less hold over your consciousness and you can become free of the bonds of the material world.

When we push forward with our consciousness into space and time, we often loose our center in the physical world. It is a selfless deed to know the future through moral imagination. To "see" the future we first must believe there is a future and that the authors of intelligent design have a "Devine Plan." We need to communicate with these timeless and spaceless beings to build the faith that there is a positive future aimed at the spiritual world. Moral imagination is a realm every human can ascend into and begin a dialogue with invisible beings using the language of the spirit. The alphabet of this language is the cosmology of the Divine Plan. Seeing how this plan has worked in the past teaches us the universal laws that will create the future. One can almost predict the future by the spiritual footprints of the past. The same beings are creating both. The difference is, human freedom must be added to the picture. The Divine Plan is already created if humans wish to accept it with total freedom, clear thinking, a pure heart, and a spiritually aligned will. But those moral actions must be done consciously and not through blind faith. A comprehensive cosmology helps develop that faith in the Divine Plan of "intelligent design" and gives us the basic alphabet to form the words and language for spiritual communion with the higher spiritual hierarchies and the Divine Trinity.

We will examine Steiner's cosmology in this booklet so that a firm foundation of gratitude to the spiritual world might engender in our souls the desire to learn the spiritual language of the Angels. We will see the cooperative sacrifices of different hierarchies as they evolve through their own human stage of spiritual development in the previous incarnations of the Earth. We will learn that each stage of evolution provides humanity with another perfected kingdom that builds the body, soul, and spirit of each human being. By analyzing the history of spiritual evolution, we will broaden our own perception of the physical world outside of us. By hearing about the different future sub-epochs, epochs, and incarnations of the Earth we will build our own personal spiritual "mansions" in a future heaven that Steiner called the Future Jupiter or New Jerusalem. Once those future heavenly kingdoms are fixed in our minds and come alive in our hearts and deeds, each person can ascend towards the future with no fear and the faith that the spiritual world is ever present to help us become love, wisdom, and goodness. Then, we shall become Angels and take flight into the spiritual worlds that always surround us beckoning us forward on the path to our spiritual self, the Holy Grail of inexhaustible grace and mercy.

What is an Angel According to Rudolf Steiner?

Nature and Spirit Beings, Part II, **Their Effects in Our Visible World**, Rudolf Steiner, Lecture X, *The Relationship between Worlds and Beings*, April 29, 1908, Munich, GA 98

"These hierarchy, in Christian esotericism, have the following names: Angels, Archangels, Archai (Primordial Forces), Powers (Elohim), Virtues (Motion/Dynamis), Dominions (Wisdom), Thrones, Cherubim, and Seraphim. These are nine different kinds of beings, to which man is connected right at the bottom of the hierarchy. Only if we look upwards beyond the realm of the Seraphim can we divine what we address as the Godhead [Holy Trinity].

The Angels, who stand one stage above the human beings, differ from them in that the mineral realm does not exist for their perception. Their perceptive faculty begins with the plant kingdom and then progresses further to the animal, the human, and to their own Angel kingdom. Within these four kingdoms, the life of the Angels takes place. What the human being perceives as a mineral filling a spatial area is for these beings empty space, blank space. The minerals do not present an obstacle for them—they are able to walk through them; they are not interested in them.

As Angelic beings, they call themselves "I." They guide and lead the eternal Ego of man. And because they, due to their nature, are able to reach down into the world of plants, they can achieve the transformation of the Earth. The Ego is regulated and led by such entities. Therefore, the naive belief that a protective being exists for the higher Ego is not unfounded. We know however, that the entities we call Angels were still human beings

11

when they were on the Old Moon. From human beings, they have evolved higher. Knowing this, it is easy to understand that man also is on the way to becoming such a higher being himself and will be one on Future Jupiter. Thus, there is something in man, that works today towards a higher existence and is on the way to become such a being. He will then be of a nature similar to such Angelic beings. Whilst the Angels guide and lead individual people through their incarnations, the Archangels lead the lives of whole groups, entire nations.

The sense organs of the Angelic beings will become understandable when I tell you that man himself has two eyes to see the mineral world with but cannot see his eyes directly on himself. The sense organs are made for perception, but they do not perceive themselves. Thus, it is with the Angels in the mineral world. Their sense organs can be found in the mineral physical world, but they do not perceive that world themselves. The sense organs of the Angels, are our precious gemstones. These are mysterious tools for Angelic beings to perceive with. Thus, these organs lie within the mineral world. In the same way that the human being has his sense of feeling and his sense of touch, these beings possess their sense of feeling, which expresses itself in the carnelian; and their facial sense in the chrysolite. They simply do not perceive within the mineral world because their sense organs are in it. Even in this regard, we can find some dim consciousness amongst the ancient people who ascribe particular properties to certain precious stones. These properties derive from the presence of Angels in them.

Just like the face of the Earth is transformed by the Angels who are guiding the human "I", and the Archangels are leading the people of nations, so the consecutive epochs are determined by the Primordial Forces (Archai-Spirits of Time). Everything that goes beyond the individual human being, that is connected to the affairs of the whole planet, are the deeds of these Powers (Elohim). The nature and weaving of the Powers is revealed to us here. They are quite correctly described in the *Bible* as the Spirits of Light or Elohim, who existed before the Earth was created. One of them is Yahweh, who forces the human beings into form. In the working and weaving of the Powers, we see what is connected to the life of the whole planet.

However, we have also already heard that certain beings always remain behind in their development. The current Powers were previously Primordial

Forces on the Moon. But there are Primordial Forces of the Moon that did not complete their set tasks and who came onto the Earth as Primordial Forces. They had not developed fast enough, although they were candidates to become Powers. The most outstanding of these Primordial Forces, who could actually be at the level of the Powers, is the entity commonly called Satan. Thus, he is at the rank of the Primordial Forces and could even be a Power."

Preparing for the Future 6th and 7th Post-Atlantean Periods

Before we can grow into an Angel, we must pass through two more Post-Atlantean Periods and two more Epochs, which Steiner often calls Post-Atlantean Epochs. We are currently in the 5th Post-Atlantean Period (Anglo-Germanic) and have two more to complete called the 6th Post-Atlantean Period (Future Russian/Slavic) and the 7th Post-Atlantean Period (Future American). After those Post-Atlantean Periods, we have two more epochs to add to human evolution: the 6th Post-Atlantean Epoch and the 7th Post-Atlantean Epoch. Some say it will take more than 30,000 years to complete the full cycle of seven Epochs before we enter a stage of dissolution and reorganization called a pralaya (period of rest). When we come forth from that "chrysalis" stage of metamorphosis, we will begin our new life as Angels. But first, we must get through the stage we are currently in which holds many trials and tribulations for the evolving human being. Many people wonder if we are in the "end times" of the apocalypse and subsequently think we will ascend to our Angel-hood after the 5th (Anglo-Germanic), 6th (Future Russian/Slavic) and 7th (Future American) Post-Atlantean Periods are completed. They might forget that we also have two more Epochs that we have to pass through: the 6th Post-Atlantean Epoch and the 7th Post Atlantean Epoch. Each of these Epochs also have seven stages of Post-Atlantean Periods to pass through (approximately 2,160 years each).

It is still a long time before we will take wing and fly to New Jerusalem as Angels. But in the meantime, every thought, feeling, and deed that we do adds to and builds the spiritual "hut", "mansion", "New Eden" in the Future Jupiter Incarnation of the Earth that we will live in. Essentially, we are creating our future Angel bodies through the moral actions we accomplish through time. Fortunately, we have time to shed our attachments to the physical world and focus our minds, our hearts, and our deeds on building the New Jerusalem in the Future Jupiter – the heavenly reward which we co-create with the spiritual hierarchy through redeeming our karma.

Decades ago, Jackson Brown wrote a song called *Before the Deluge* that clearly described the longings of his generation to "seek peace not war" and to "go back to the land" in true millennialist's fashion. It was a cry for help to the divine to bestow mercy on those who wish to preserve, respect, and cherish Mother Nature. Their longing for that which "comes down from the sky", like New Jerusalem, is the mood of soul that arises as an awakened initiate approaches the threshold between the physical and spiritual worlds. These yearnings for the spirit to descend from heaven into the prepared "heart of longing" of each individual is a necessary prerequisite to properly approach the Dweller of the Threshold and the unseen world beyond. Jackson Brown was promoting an imagination of building a bio-ark with Mother Nature to weather the storm and ride out the deluge that he believed was coming soon. He describes this longing for mercy in the lyrics of his song:

Before the Deluge
by Jackson Brown

Some of them were dreamers

And some of them were fools

Who were making plans and thinking of the future

With the energy of the innocent

They were gathering the tools

They would need to make their journey back to nature

While the sand slipped through the opening

And their hands reached for the golden ring

With their hearts they turned to each other's hearts for refuge

In the troubled years that came before the deluge

Some of them knew pleasure

And some of them knew pain

And for some of them it was only the moment that mattered

And on the brave and crazy wings of youth

They went flying around in the rain

And their feathers, once so fine, grew torn and tattered

And in the end they traded their tired wings

For the resignation that living brings

And exchanged love's bright and fragile glow

For the glitter and the rouge

And in a moment they were swept before the deluge

Let the music keep our spirits high

Let the buildings keep our children dry

Let creation reveal its secrets by and by, by and by

When the light that's lost within us reaches the sky

Some of them were angry

At the way the Earth was abused

By the men who learned how to forge her beauty into power

And they struggled to protect her from them

Only to be confused

By the magnitude of her fury in the final hour

And when the sand was gone and the time arrived

In the naked dawn only a few survived

And in attempts to understand a thing so simple and so huge

Believed that they were meant to live after the deluge

Let the music keep our spirits high

Let the buildings keep our children dry

Let creation reveal its secrets by and by, by and by

When the light that's lost within us reaches the sky

The soul mood of redemption from the apocalypse is beautifully described in these lyrics. As Brown says, "In the naked dawn only a few survived", while the others met the fate that "in a moment they were swept before the deluge." In every apocalypse there is always a small remnant who survive through the grace and mercy of the divine. Some type of "ark" carries them to the new home, called in the *Book of Revelation,* the "new heaven and new Earth."

Everyone desires to know their destiny, and often people fear what is coming to meet them from the unknown offerings of the future. Even the ancient gods feared and respected the three Fates (Norns) who spun, measured, and cut the thread of life for gods and humans. We all tremble on the threshold with fear and trepidation at the many times we have been selfish and lacked love for God, our neighbors, and ourselves. Truly in our times, the 'deluge' is upon us all and we need to be ready to step forward into divine salvation, or backward into miserable drowning from the overwhelming deluge. It all depends on whether we had previously prepared our "ark of consciousness" to weather the waves of judgment and tribulation and if we had developed the faith, hope, and love to enkindle the bright dawn of a better day.

Rudolf Steiner tells us about the nature of the future in his cosmology which informs us that we are presently in the Fifth Post-Atlantean Period (sub-epoch, era or age of civilization). During this age, the outer world will look like the 'war of all-against-all' has arrived and only faith in the divine world and its spiritual beings, as well as your own developing spiritual self, can ride-out the ravages of the stormy deluge of the material world that wishes to drown the spirit. It is love that builds the edifices of the future that we all inherit, the many 'mansions' in the heavenly kingdom that Christ spoke about. Every conscious free-deed of love builds that spiritual edifice of love in the world of the future—Future Jupiter. We each inherent our self-created "mansion" as our new spiritual body that carries the moral thoughts, feelings, and deeds offered to the Holy Trinity and the Diving Spiritual Hierarchy from life to life.

The Sixth Post-Atlantean Period will begin after 3,573 AD. During that Period, it will be Love that guides and leads humanity to a direct encounter with the Cosmic Christ. Sophia, or Anthroposophia as Steiner calls her, will be an ever-present consciousness of wisdom found in nature which is available for continuous communication with spiritually awakened humanity. Christ, the Being of Love, will also be directly available to awakened human consciousness as a higher development of the expression of the human conscience. The conscience of the individual will be in direct communication with Christ, who will act as a higher aspect of the human soul that is spiritual and eternal. In the future, Christ will illumine for the soul and spirit the karmic consequences of each human thought, feeling, and deed. The refined parts of what Rudolf Steiner called the Consciousness Soul will become the Spiritual Soul, a type of higher ego of the physical world that will be able to speak and communicate with the individual's Spirit-Self through Manasic thinking, that is also called Moral Imagination. This type of Moral Imagination is a direct form of communication with beings who live in the realm of Angels.

The best descriptions of the Sixth Post-Atlantean Period are found throughout the works of Rudolf Steiner. In an effort to illuminate the nature of the future as an antidote to the fear and terror of what comes towards us from the future, we share Steiner's indications that tell us to develop faith, love, and hope in the 5th, 6th, and 7th Periods to gain the wisdom and insight to fulfill the mission of human spiritual development. It is not fear that should motivate us, but instead it should be the faith in the ever-present help of the spiritual world that is filled with wisdom and gives pure love freely, the august master-binding of all.

The Great Cycles of Seven

The mystery of the seven stars from *Revelation* indicates the cycles of creation that are called rounds, globes, incarnations of Earth, and other nomenclature that Rudolf Steiner names Old Saturn, Old Sun, Old Moon, Earth, Future Jupiter, Future Venus, Future Vulcan. Within those seven cycles (rounds) are smaller cycles of seven called Epochs: Polarian, Hyperborean, Lemurian, Atlantean, 5th Post-Atlantean, 6th Post-Atlantean, 7th Post-Atlantean. Within those Epochs are seven smaller 2,160 year cycles called Periods: Ancient Indian, Ancient Perian, Egyptian/Babylonian, Greco/Roman, Anglo/Germanic, Future Russian, Future American. Thus, we have 7 x 7 x 7 = 343 cycles for a complete creation cycle. (Diagram

Foundations of Esotericism, Rudolf Steiner, Lecture XXIV, Oct 26, 1905, GA 93a

Incarnation		Consciousness
Old Saturn	=	Deep trance-consciousness
Old Sun	=	Dreamless sleep-consciousness
Old Moon	=	Dreaming sleep or picture consciousness
Earth	=	Waking consciousness or awareness of objects
Future Jupiter	=	Psychic or conscious picture-consciousness
Future Venus	=	Super-psychic or conscious life-consciousness
Future Vulcan	=	Spiritual or self-conscious universal consciousness

Rounds or Globes	Body Developed
Old Saturn	Physical Body
Old Sun	Etheric Body
Old Moon	Astral Body
Earth	Ego ("I Am")
Future Jupiter	Spirit-Self–Manas
Future Venus	Life-Spirit–Buddhi
Future Vulcan	Spirit Human–Atman

The Apocalypse of St. John, Rudolf Steiner, Lecture VIII, June 25, 1908, Nuremberg, GA 104

Ages of Civilization

I	II	III	IV	V	VI	VIII
				1 2 3 4 5 6 7		
				a-------b		

"Thus, if we represent it in a diagram, we have our seven ages of civilization in the space between the letters a–b, so that we have the ancient Indian civilization as the first, the ancient Persian as the second, the Assyrian-Babylonian-Chaldean-Egyptian-Jewish, the Graeco-Latin, and our own as the fifth stage of the post-Atlantean epoch. The [figure above] would be the Atlantean epoch, (a) the great flood by which this comes to an end, and (b) the great War of All against All. Then follows an epoch of seven stages (VI) which is represented by the seven seals, then follows another (VII) also containing seven stages, represented by the seven trumpets. Here again lies the boundary of our physical Earth development.

Now the Atlantean civilization (IV), which preceded our own, was also preceded by other stages of civilization; for that of our own (V), which follows the Atlantean, is the Fifth-Stage on our Earth. Four stages of civilization preceded it. But we can scarcely call the first stage a civilization culture. Everything was still etheric and spiritual, all in such a condition that if it had developed further in this way, it would not have become visible at all to sense organs such as ours. The first stage developed when the Sun was still bound up with our Earth. There were then quite different conditions, one could not speak of anything which looked like the objects now surrounding us. Then followed a stage characterized by the Sun separating. Then one characterized by the Moon leaving the Earth; this was the third stage, which we call the ancient Lemurian. At this point the present man appeared on our Earth in his very first form, concerning which I have pointed out that they were such grotesque bodily forms that it would shock you if you were to hear them described. After the Lemurian followed the Atlantean, and finally our own."

Seven Epochs of Earth

Polarian Epoch
Hyperborean Epoch
Lemurian Epoch
Atlantean Epoch

5th Post-Atlantean Epoch	7,227 BC	– 7,894 AD
6th Post-Atlantean Epoch	7,894 AD	– 23,014 AD
7th Post-Atlantean Epoch	23,014 AD	– 38,134 AD

5th Post-Atlantean Periods (Cultural Periods or Ages of Civilization)

Ancient Indian Period	(7,227-5,097 BC)	Cancer	Etheric Body
Ancient Persian Period	(5,067-2,907 BC)	Gemini	Astral Body
Egyptian-Chaldean Period	(2,907-747 BC)	Taurus	Sentient Soul
Greco-Latin Period	(747 BC-1,413 AD)	Aries	Intellectual Soul
Anglo-Germanic Period	(1,413-3,573 AD)	Pisces	Consciousness Soul
Russian-Slavic Period	(3,573-5,733 AD)	Aquarius	Spirit-Self (nascent)
American Period	(5,733-7,894 AD)	Capricorn	Life-Spirit (nascent)

Each of these cycles of seven follows a characteristic pattern of a septenary pendulum swing that begins building momentum in stages 1, 2, and 3, to the full momentum during stage 4, and then the accumulated force of the momentum carrying thru 5 and 6, with a decline in momentum in stage 7. We also see in the natural metamorphosis of evolution that stage 1 is repeated, at a higher level, during stage 7, stage 2 in 6, stage 3 in 5. Rudolf Steiner tells us that the first half of Earth evolution was called the Mars half while the second half is called the Mercury half of evolution with the middle being defined by what he called "The Turning Point of Time", the "Mystery of Golgotha"—i.e., the birth, death, and resurrection of Jesus Christ. (See Diagrams 1 – 6 in Appendix.)

```
    1        7
     2      6
      3   5
       4
```

Each of the seven stages of evolution has a special task. The task of furthering evolution comes from planting the new seed of development that occurs in the 4th stage and seeing it begin to come to fruition during the 5th stage. Physical, cultural, and spiritual evolution and innovation are created during the 5th stage of this cycle of seven, the leading edge of evolution. We find this to be true whether we are examining great or small cycles of time; five is the number of change and the new impulse of evolution. Certain archetypal aspects and characteristics repeat themselves like a tessellating fractal in the morphology of development. The signatures of the cycle of seven stages can help the historian analyze the effects of the creative hierarchies as they manifest through rhythmic cycles of time that relate to the rulership periods of different hierarchical beings. For example, the seven major Archai (Time Spirits) each rule for around 300-354 years, comprising a period of time that is close to the 2,160 years of a Post-Atlantean Period as a cycle coinciding with seven Archai ruler-ships. Seven periods of 2,160 years comprise an Epoch of 15,120 years. On the other hand, when twelve Periods have passed, a full cycle of 25,920 years, the Platonic Great Year, will have complete a precession of the equinox backwards through the twelve signs of the Zodiac. These cycles are taught by Rudolf Steiner to reveal the Divine Plan of creation as it links with solar, planetary, and celestial cycles. They also relate to human breathing and heart rhythms.

The Apocalypse of St. John, Rudolf Steiner, Lecture IX, June 26, 1908, Nuremberg, GA 104

"We have seen that we pass through 343 conditions of form. Now, the subject grows more complicated when we learn that the matter does not end here, but that man must also pass through various conditions with each condition of form. In our mineral condition of life during the Earth period three conditions of form have preceded the present physical condition of form and three others will follow it. But now the physical again passes through seven conditions, and these are the seven of which we have spoken in previous lectures; the first when the Sun is still united with the Earth, the second when it separates, the third when the Moon withdraws, the fourth that of the Atlantean humanity. The Atlantean humanity lives in the fourth epoch of the development of the physical condition of form. Thus, within each condition of form you have again seven epochs or so-called root-races, although the expression "race" applies only to the middle condition. We are now living in the fifth epoch, the post-Atlantean epoch, between the great Atlantean flood and the great War of All against All. The sixth will follow this and then the seventh. The sixth epoch is indicated in the Apocalypse of John by the seven seals, and the seventh by the seven trumpets. Then the Earth passes over into the astral. That is a new condition of form which again will have its seven epochs.

And still our diagram is not at an end. Each epoch as it runs its course between such events as the great Atlantean flood and the great War of All against All must again be divided into seven ages. As regards the fifth epoch there are the Indian age of civilization, the Persian age of civilization, the Assyrian-Babylonian-Chaldean-Egyptian-Jewish age, the Graeco-Latin age, our own age, then the sixth, which is indicated in the Apocalypse by the community of Philadelphia, and the seventh age of civilization which will follow that."

Cosmic Memory, The Earth and Its Future, Rudolf Steiner, Chapter 13, GA 11

"Life proceeds with the greatest speed on Old Saturn, the rapidity then decreases on the Old Sun, becomes still less on the Old Moon and reaches its slowest phase on the Earth. On the latter it becomes slower and slower, to the point at which self-consciousness develops. Then the speed increases again. Therefore, today man has already passed the time of the greatest slowness of his development. Life has begun to accelerate again. On Future Jupiter the speed of the Old Moon, on Future Venus that of the Old Sun will again be attained. The last planet which can still be counted among the series of Earthly transformations, and hence follows Future Venus, is called Future Vulcan by mystery science. On this planet the provisional goal of the development of mankind is attained. The condition of consciousness into which man enters there is called piety or spiritual consciousness. Man will attain it in the seventh cycle of Future Vulcan after a repetition of the six preceding stages. Not much can be publicly communicated about life on this planet. In mystery science one speaks of it in such a way that it is said, 'No soul which, with its thinking still tied to a physical body, should reflect about Future Vulcan and its life.' That is, only the mystery students of the higher order, who may leave their physical body and can acquire supersensible knowledge outside of it, can learn something about Future Vulcan."

Spiritual Hierarchies, Rudolf Steiner, Lecture 5, GA 110

"The course of evolution is this: a Sun, which from the beginning is included in such a system, has at first to throw off its planets, being too weak to develop further without excluding them. It grows strong, absorbs its planets again, and grows into a Future Vulcan. Then the whole is dissolved, and from the Future Vulcan globe is formed a hollow globe which is something like the circles of Thrones, Cherubim, and Seraphim. The Sun will thus dissolve in space, sacrifice itself, send forth its Being into the Universe, and through this will itself become a circle of Beings like the Thrones, Cherubim, Seraphim, which will then advance towards new creation."

Reading the Pictures of the Apocalypse, Rudolf Steiner, Lecture XII, Kristiania, 1909, GA 104a

"In the age represented by the seven seals something like a shower of meteorites will occur, caused by increasing materialism, and some human beings will ascend to a spiritual state. What the spiritualized human beings have acquired through their efforts in our Post-Atlantean Age will completely permeate them within. When, in the age of the sixth seal, everything that the human being has in terms of sentient soul, intellectual soul, and consciousness soul has been worked into the other members, human beings will have achieved the ability to create an external imprint of their inner life in their gesture, features, in their whole life. Because they have worked on their development, they will be able in the fourth, fifth, and sixth ages in the epoch of the seals, to use these three soul forces—the sentient, intellectual, and consciousness souls—to permeate and work on themselves in order to take in manas."

Charts Derived from the Works of Rudolf Steiner:

The Seven Virtues and Vices

Virtue	Classic Virtue	Vice	Description	Proverbs
Humility	Courage	Pride	Obedience	Wisdom
Love	Charity	Envy	Kindness	Understanding
Purity	Prudence	Lust	Chastity	Strength
Generosity	Justice	Greed	Benevolence	Honor/Riches
Temperance	Temperance	Gluttony	Self-control	Judgment
Diligence	Hope	Sloth	Persistence	Righteousness
Patience	Faith	Anger	Patience	Counsel

The Holy Trinity—Father/Son/HolySpirit

Dionysius	Spirits of	Planet	Donation	Offspring
Seraphim	Love	Saturn	Fire reflection	Rotation of time
Cherubim	Harmony	Jupiter	Air reflection	Elementary Spirts
Thrones	Will	Mars	Water reflection	Group soul/mineral
Kyriotetes	Wisdom	Sun	Life ether	Group soul/plants
Dynamis	Motion	Sun	Sound ether	Group soul/animals
Exusiai	Form	Sun	Light ether	Group soul of man
Archai	Personality	Mercury	Warmth etheric	Nature Spirits/earth
Archangels	Sons of Fire	Venus	Air etheric	Nature Spirits/water
Angels	S. Twilight	Moon	Water etheric	Nature Spirits/air

The Holy Trinity—Father/Son/HolySpirit

Dionysius	Sense	Body	Aristotle	Sign	Center
Seraphim	Ego	Spirit Man	Being	Gemini	Sun
Cherubim	Touch	Life Spirit	Suffering	Cancer	Sun
Thrones	Life	Spirit Self	Activity	Leo	Sun
Kyriotetes	Movement	Spiritual Soul	Position	Virgo	Sun
Dynamis	Balance	Intellectual Soul	Time	Libra	Sun
Exusiai	Smell	Sentient Soul	Space	Scorpio	Sun
Archai	Taste	Astral	Relation	Sagittarius	Earth
Archangels	Sight	Etheric	Quality	Capricorn	Earth
Angels	Warmth	Physical	Quantity	Aquarius	Earth

The Holy Trinity—Father/Son/HolySpirit

Dionysius	Activity	Field	Nature	Domain	After Death
Seraphim	Matter	Solar system	Love	Zodiac	
Cherubim	Matter	Solar system	Harmony	Zodiac	
Thrones	Matter	Solar system	Willpower	Saturn	Physical Body
Kyriotetes	Etheric	Solar system	Sophia	Jupiter	Creation of Limbs
Dynamis	Etheric	Each planet	Dynamism	Mars	Creation of Head
Exusiai	Etheric	Sun	Christ	Sun	Relation to Humanity
Archai	Souls	Mercury	Intuition	Mercury	Relation to Religion
Archangels	Souls	Venus	Inspiration	Venus	Morality Developed
Angels	Souls	Moon	Imagination	Moon	Experience Kamaloca

Archangelic Regencies as Time Spirits and Revelations

According to Johannes Trithemius of Sponheim (1462-1516), in his book *Concerning the Seven Spiritual Intelligences, Who, After God, Actuate the Universe,* the Seven Archangelic Spirits each rule in turn for a regency of 354 years and four months. Rudolf Steiner approximates this to 300-350 years for each Archangelic period. Each Archangel rises into the rank of Archai (Spirits of Time) for the period they rule and then, usually, go back into the realm of the Archangels. Our current Time Spirit (Spirit of the Age or Zeitgeist) is the Archai Michael who shall remain an Archai after his rulership as an Archai has ended; and as a result of this, the Archangel Vidar has assumed the role of the Sun Archangel replacing Michael as the Sun Archangel since November, 1879 when Michael ascended to the stage of an Archai. A ruling Archai leads humanity for a period of 2,160 years, which constitutes a Cultural Period (sub-epoch or Age of Civilization) and is approximately the total of the seven Archangelic Regencies.

Archangelic Regencies as Archai (Time Spirits)

Michael	(Sun)	725 BC–200 BC
Oriphiel	(Saturn)	200 BC–150 AD
Anael	(Venus)	150 AD–500 AD
Zachariel	(Jupiter)	500 AD–850 AD
Raphael	(Mercury)	850 AD–1,190 AD
Samael	(Mars)	1,190 AD–1,510 AD
Gabriel	(Moon)	1,510 AD–1,879 AD
Michael	(Sun)	1,879 AD–2,233 AD
Oriphiel	(Saturn)	2,235 AD–2,589 AD

Michael (Sun) 725 BC–200 BC: Graeco-Roman period, Persian invasions, Athenian politics, Socrates, Plato, Aristotle, Alexander the Great.

Oriphiel (Saturn) 200 BC–150 AD: Savage and crude behavior leading to suffering. Bestows pain to show that we may learn from our sins. The Crucifixion of Christ.

Anael (Venus) 150 AD–500: Relearn the gentle ways of the soul. Buddhism in China, Mayan Civilization.

Zachariel (Jupiter) 500 AD–850: Development of civilization, separation of ideologies and beliefs. Disintegration of Roman Empire and growth of Christianity, founding of Islam.

Raphael (Mercury) 850 AD–1190: Invention and knowledge development. Raphael is considered the protector of the Tree of Life. He governs the healing powers at work in our organism and is the Spring spirit that circles the Earth. During autumn he creates the forces of human breathing and anchors his healing powers in it. The Golden Age of Arab Culture especially medicine, founding of Russia, strong Papacy.

Samael (Mars) 1190 AD–1510: Changes in government, monarchy, religions, castes, laws, and civil rulership. Associated with martial aspects. Viking invasion of Europe, Muslims in Jerusalem, Genghis Khan, Crusades, Christopher Columbus, Middle Ages.

Gabriel (Moon) 1510 AD–1879: Development of virtue, arts, and childbirth. He is regarded as a messenger of God and is often seen as an interpreter of visions. Has a special relationship to the astral body of man and the Old Moon incarnation of the Earth. Worked on the development of a new organ in man's brain by regulating human births and raises the powers of the Intellectual Soul to the level of the Consciousness Soul. Renaissance, Victorian Age.

Michael (Sun) 1879 AD–2233: Inner and outer awakenings, cosmic wisdom, and containment of evil. Promotes the Earth's development in the service of the Christ in such a way that the human I can unfold as richly as possible. WWI and II, hippies, esoteric movements, industrial revolution. *"As formerly Man could speak of Jahve-Michael, the leader of the age, so now we can speak the Christ-Michael. Michael has been exalted to a higher stage: from Folk Spirit to Time Spirit, inasmuch as from being the Messenger of Jahve he has become the Messenger of Christ."* GA 152

Oriphiel (Saturn) 2235 AD–2589: "Oriphiel is the one who must come to shake humankind, to jolt it through terrifying suffering, awakening it to its true vocation. In four to six centuries the small group of men who are being prepared today will serve the God Oriphiel so that mankind can be saved. But when dark powers rage most terribly, the brightest light also shines. Oriphiel has ruled before during the time when Christ appeared on Earth as evil powers of degeneration and decadence were ruling everywhere on Earth. Oriphiel is called the Archangel of wrath, who purifies mankind with a strong hand as a particularly bright light must always arise in especially dark times. Christ was born in the Oriphiel age and when Oriphiel rules again the spiritual light that was brought by Christian Rosenkreutz, and is now being spread, must have generated a host of clairvoyant men who are pioneers working consciously towards a goal. This will produce a separation into good and evil races. Then good will develop into a divine good, and evil into a terrible Antichrist. Then every one of us needs world helpers and all the strength that he can only gain through the overcoming of suffering and evil. Divine love appears in the form of divine wrath in the sphere of human illusions." GA 266

The Seven Letters to the Churches the Seven Great Rounds

Spiritual Science teaches us that the Seven Letters to the Churches from *Revelation* are indeed addressing the seven Post-Atlantean Periods [Sub-Epochs or Ages of Civilization]: *Ephesus* (Ancient India), *Smyrna* (Ancient Persia), *Pergamos* (Egypt/ Babylon/Chaldea), *Thyatira* (Greek/Roman), *Sardis* (Anglo-Germanic), *Philadelphia* (Future Russian/Slavic), *Laodicea* (Future American). Thus, we are currently in the 5th Post-Atlantean Period associated with Sardis. The future 6th Post-Atlantean Period is related to Philadelphia while the 7th Post-Atlantean Period is related to Laodicea. It is easy to see the corollaries between the Seven Letters to the Churches in *Revelation* compared to the seven Post-Atlantean Periods. Therefore, the 6th and 7th letters tell us about the future of humanity that needs to unfold before humans evolve into budding Angels. *Revelation* describes the power of the messages to the seven churches and the beneficial outcomes of those who are faithful in the following words:

> "The mystery of the seven stars which thou sawest in my right hand, and the seven golden candlesticks. The seven stars are the Angels of the seven churches: and the seven candlesticks which thou sawest are the seven churches." (*Revelation* 1:20)

He that hath an ear, let him hear what the Spirit saith unto the churches; To him that overcometh will I give to eat of the tree of life, which is in the midst of the paradise of God." (*Revelation* 2:7)

"He that hath an ear, let him hear what the Spirit saith unto the churches; To him that overcometh will I give to eat of the tree of life, which is in the midst of the paradise of God." (*Revelation* 2:7)

"He that hath an ear, let him hear what the Spirit saith unto the churches; He that overcometh shall not be hurt of the second death." (*Revelation* 2:11)

"He that hath an ear, let him hear what the Spirit saith unto the churches; To him that overcometh will I give to eat of the hidden manna, and will give him a white stone, and in the stone a new name written, which no man knoweth saving he that receiveth it." (*Revelation* 2:17)

"Him that overcometh will I make a pillar in the temple of my God, and he shall go no more out: and I will write upon him the name of my God, and the name of the city of my God, which is New Jerusalem, which cometh down out of heaven from my God: and I will write upon him my new name." (*Revelation* 3:12)

"To him that overcometh will I grant to sit with me in my throne, even as I also overcame, and am set down with my Father in his throne." (*Revelation* 3:21)

Advice to the Seven Churches

1. *Ephesus*—Ancient India—"I know thy works, and thy labor, and thy patience, and how thou canst not bear them which are evil: and thou hast tried them which say they are apostles, and are not, and hast found them liars: And hast borne, and hast patience, and for my name's sake hast labored, and hast not fainted. Nevertheless, I have somewhat against thee because thou hast left thy first love. Remember therefore from whence thou art fallen, and repent, and

do the first works; or else I will come unto thee quickly, and will remove thy candlestick out of his place, except thou repent." (*Revelation* 2:2-6)

2. *Smyrna*—Ancient Persia—"I know thy works, and tribulation, and poverty, (but thou art rich), Fear none of those things which thou shalt suffer: behold, the devil shall cast some of you into prison, that ye may be tried; and ye shall have tribulation ten days: be thou faithful unto death, and I will give thee a crown of life." (*Revelation* 2:9-10)

3. *Pergamos*—Egypt/Babylon/Chaldea—"I know thy works, and where thou dwellest, even where Satan's seat is… But I have a few things against thee, because thou hast there them that hold the doctrine of Balaam, who taught Balac to cast a stumbling-block before the children of Israel, to eat things sacrificed unto idols, and to commit fornication. Repent; or else I will come unto thee quickly and will fight against them with the sword of my mouth.

4. *Thyatira*—Greek/Roman—"I know thy works, and charity, and service, and faith, and thy patience, and thy works; and the last to be more than the first. Notwithstanding I have a few things against thee, because thou sufferest that woman Jezebel, which calleth herself a prophetess, to teach and to seduce my servants to commit fornication, and to eat things sacrificed unto idols. And I gave her space to repent of her fornication; and she repented not. Behold, I will cast her into a bed, and them that commit adultery with her into great tribulation, except they repent of their deeds. And I will kill her children with death; and all the churches shall know that I am he which searcheth the reins and hearts: and I will give unto every one of you according to your works. But unto you I say, and unto the rest in Thyatira, as many as have not this doctrine, and which have not known the depths of Satan, as they speak; I will put upon you none other burden. But that which ye have already hold fast till I come. And he that overcometh, and keepeth my works unto the end, to him will I give power over the nations: And he shall rule them with a rod of iron; as the vessels of a potter shall they be broken to shivers: even as I received of my Father. And I will give him the morning star." (*Revelation* 2:19-28)

5. *Sardis*—Anglo-Germanic—"Be watchful, and strengthen the things which remain, that are ready to die: for I have not found thy works perfect before God. Remember therefore how thou hast received and heard, and hold fast, and repent. If therefore thou shalt not watch, I will come on thee as a thief, and thou shalt not know what hour I will come upon thee. Thou hast a few names even

in Sardis which have not defiled their garments; and they shall walk with me in white: for they are worthy. He that overcometh, the same shall be clothed in white raiment; and I will not blot out his name out of the book of life, but I will confess his name before my Father, and before his Angels." (*Revelation* 3:2-5)

6. *Philadelphia*—Future Russian/Slavic—"I know thy works: behold, I have set before thee an open door, and no man can shut it: for thou hast a little strength, and hast kept my word, and hast not denied my name. Behold, I will make them of the synagogue of Satan, which say they are Jews, and are not, but do lie; behold, I will make them to come and worship before thy feet, and to know that I have loved thee. Because thou hast kept the word of my patience, I also will keep thee from the hour of temptation, which shall come upon all the world, to try them that dwell upon the Earth. Behold, I come quickly: hold that fast which thou hast, that no man take thy crown." (*Revelation* 3:8-11)

7. *Laodicea*—Future American—"I know thy works, that thou art neither cold nor hot: I would thou wert cold or hot. So then because thou art lukewarm, and neither cold nor hot, I will spue thee out of my mouth. Because thou sayest, I am rich, and increased with goods, and have need of nothing; and knowest not that thou art wretched, and miserable, and poor, and blind, and naked: I counsel thee to buy of me gold tried in the fire, that thou mayest be rich; and white raiment, that thou mayest be clothed, and that the shame of thy nakedness do not appear; and anoint thine eyes with eye-salve, that thou mayest see. As many as I love, I rebuke and chasten: be zealous therefore, and repent. Behold, I stand at the door, and knock: if any man hear my voice, and open the door, I will come in to him, and will sup with him, and he with me." (*Revelation* 3:15-20)

The Seven Bowls of Wrath of Apocalypse 5th Post-Atlantean Period

Rudolf Steiner tells us that the 5th Post-Atlantean Epoch, of 15,120 years, begins with the Great Flood of Atlantis and ends with the War of All against All. We are now in the 5th Post-Atlantean Period (2,160-year Sub-Epoch; Anglo-Germanic). We have two more 2,160 Post-Atlantean Periods until the War of All against All. There will be a recapitulation at a higher level of the War of All against All after the 15,120-year long 6th and 7th Epochs that is called by Rudolf Steiner "The Revolution (Upheaval) of the Elements." By the time of the "Revolution-Upheaval", the Moon will have united with the Earth and the two will then unite with the Sun. Afterwards, a great pralaya will happen; whereby, the Earth will be transformed into an Astral Globe and then later will undergo a further metamorphosis into a Heavenly Realm, that is called in the East, "Devachan." Then as Rudolf Steiner said, all physical aspects of Earth will dissolve like "salt crystals in water." After the 6th and 7th Epochs, the Future Jupiter condition of the "Earth" will manifest.

During the 5th Post-Atlantean Period, humans resemble the characteristics that Saint John used to describe the church of Sardis. Rudolf Steiner points out that our current 2,160-year 5th Sub-Period (Anglo-Germanic) will experience the vials of wrath brought by the seven Angels. These plagues of tribulation test the souls of the faithful as God's wrath is visited on the 5th (Anglo-Germanic), 6th (Russian), and 7th (American) Post-Atlantean Periods; and as we indicated earlier, around 8000 AD Rudolf Steiner predicts that the Moon will begin to break apart and fall towards the Earth.

1. *The First Angel* went and poured out his bowl on the land, and ugly, festering sores broke out on the people who had the mark of the beast and worshiped its image.

2. *The Second Angel* poured out his bowl on the sea, and it turned into blood like that of a dead person, and every living thing in the sea died.

3. *The Third Angel* poured out his bowl on the rivers and springs of water, and they became blood.

4. *The Fourth Angel* poured out his bowl on the Sun, and the Sun was allowed to scorch people with fire. They were seared by the intense heat, and they cursed the name of God, who had control over these plagues, but they refused to repent and glorify him.

5. *The Fifth Angel* poured out his bowl on the throne of the beast, and its kingdom was plunged into darkness. People gnawed their tongues in agony and cursed the God of heaven because of their pains and their sores, but they refused to repent of what they had done.

6. *The Sixth Angel* poured out his bowl on the great river Euphrates, and its water was dried up to prepare the way for the kings from the East. Then I saw three impure spirits that looked like frogs; they came out of the mouth of the dragon, out of the mouth of the beast and out of the mouth of the false prophet. They are demonic spirits that perform signs, and they go out to the kings of the whole world, to gather them for the battle on the great day of God Almighty. "Look,

I come like a thief! Blessed is the one who stays awake and remains clothed, so as not to go naked and be shamefully exposed." Then they gathered the kings together to the place that in Hebrew is called Armageddon.

7. *The Seventh Angel* poured out his bowl into the air, and out of the temple came a loud voice from the throne, saying, "It is done!" Then there came flashes of lightning, rumblings, peals of thunder and a severe Earthquake. No Earthquake like it has ever occurred since mankind has been on Earth, so tremendous was the quake. The great city split into three parts, and the cities of the nations collapsed. God remembered Babylon the Great and gave her the cup filled with the wine of the fury of his wrath. Every island fled away, and the mountains could not be found. From the sky huge hailstones, each weighing about a hundred pounds, fell on people. And they cursed God on account of the plague of hail because the plague was so terrible.

The Seven Seals of *Apocalypse* 6th Post-Atlantean Period

As we move towards the Future Russian/Slavic Sixth Post-Atlantean Period of 2,160 years, it is good to know what to expect and what great transformations will happen in the metamorphosis of the human being. Rudolf Steiner has pointed out that the Future Russian/Slavic Sixth Post-Atlantean Period will go through seven stages that in turn correlate to the Seven Seals of the Apocalypse. He also describes, in great detail, what that coming future 6th Post-Atlantean Period will look like. It light of this, we have gathered 39 statements about the Future Russian/Slavic Sixth Post-Atlantean Period – Philadelphia – from Rudolf Steiner's lectures and presented them below. This list will indicate what each person needs to work towards in order to evolve into the next stage of humanity; toward what Rudolf Steiner referred to as the spirits of freedom and love as a necessary stage of development leading to the attainment of Angel-hood in the Future Jupiter planetary condition (globe). From *Revelation* we hear the author describe these stages in the following images:

1. *The First Seal: White Horse*—As the Savior breaks the first seal of the great book, a wondrous scene flashes before the gaze of the holy apostle John, He says, "And I looked, and behold, a white horse. He who sat on it had a bow; and a crown was given to him, and he went out conquering and to conquer." (*Revelation* 6:2) In the first seal we see Christ with the wreath of a conqueror. He rides the white horse, white being the emblem of victory and also of purity.

2. *The Second Seal: Red Horse*—"When He opened the second seal, I heard the second living creature saying, 'Come and see.' Another horse, fiery red, went out. And it was granted to the one who sat on it to take peace from the Earth, and that people should kill one another; and there was given to him a great sword." (*Revelation* 6:3, 4)

3. *The Third Seal: Black Horse*—"The third seal was broken, and the apostle says, "When He opened the third seal, I heard the third living creature say, 'Come and see.' So I looked, and behold, a black horse, and he who sat on it had a pair of scales in his hand." (*Revelation* 6:5, 6)

4. *The Fourth Seal: Pale Horse*—"When He opened the fourth seal, I heard the voice of the fourth living creature saying, 'Come and see.' So I looked, and behold, a pale horse. And the name of him who sat on it was Death, and Hades followed with him. And power was given to them over a fourth of the Earth, to kill with sword, with hunger, with death, and by the beasts of the Earth." (*Revelation* 6:7, 8)

5. *The Fifth Seal: Souls Crying Out Under The Altar*—"When He opened the fifth seal, I saw under the altar the souls of those who had been slain for the word of God and for the testimony which they held. And they cried with a loud voice, saying, 'How long, O Lord, holy and true, until You judge and avenge our blood on those who dwell on the Earth?' Then a white robe was given to each of them; and it was said to them that they should rest a little while longer, until both the number of their fellow servants and their brethren, who would be killed as they were, was completed." (*Revelation* 6:9-11)

6. *The Sixth Seal: Earthquake, Sun, and Moon*—"I looked when He opened the sixth seal, and behold, there was a great Earthquake; and the Sun became black as sackcloth of hair, and the Moon became like blood. And the stars of heaven fell to the Earth, as a fig tree drops its late figs when it is shaken by a mighty wind. Then the sky receded as a scroll when it is rolled up, and every mountain and island was moved out of its place. And the kings of the Earth, the great men, the rich men, the commanders, the mighty men, every slave and every free man, hid themselves in the caves and in the rocks of the mountains." (*Revelation* 6:12-15)

7. *The Seventh Seal: Silence in Heaven*—"When He opened the seventh seal, there was silence in heaven for about half an hour." (*Revelation* 8:1)

The Future Russian/ Slavic Sixth Period

These are the characteristics of the Future Sixth Post-Atlantean Period (Russian/Slavic Sub-Epoch) of 2,160 years that are described by Rudolf Steiner throughout numerous lecture cycles. Understanding these "predictions" of what is to come prepares the aspirant for the future and indicates what they should be working on in the present. These are the steps up the mountain of spiritual development, the rungs of the ladder to heaven. The aspirant is well-advised to aim their personal spiritual development towards these ideals as they unfold their wings through moral development.

Predictions about the Future Russian/Slavic 6th Post-Atlantean Period and Beyond

1. Will be preceded by mighty cataclysms and physical catastrophes

2. Will bring genius, clairvoyance, and the creative spirit

3. Will be just as spiritual as our age is materialistic

4. Humans will be led by themselves, by the light of their own souls

5. Brotherliness prevails, freedom of thought, and pneumatology (Spirit-Self)

6. Will bring Peace and Brotherhood through a common Wisdom

7. Will experience the suffering of another human being as their own suffering

8. Science will be antiquated superstition replaced by spiritual knowledge

9. Russian soul feels the Spirit-Self descend through community

10. Kindles love for everything in existence

11. Physical body will become a faithful copy of the etheric

12. Humanity shall gradually discover the etheric

13. Christianity will appear in its perfected form

14. Human features will be marked for good or evil; whereby one's morality, or lack of it will be written on the face and the body

15. Good or evil on tendencies are revealed on the forehead and through gestures, movements of hands – so that they represent the beauty or ugliness of soul

16. Bring goodness out of evil through a process of spiritual alchemy

17. Vegetarianism flourishes; thereby discarding meat-eating as barbaric

18. The beholding the etheric Christ will steadily increase

19. Thoughts will ring forth outwardly

20. Good people will bear in their countenance the impression of Christ Jesus, as is revealed through the qualities of their words and thoughts

21. Ripest fruit will appear in the 6th Period with understanding for the spiritual world

22. The challenge will be to draw in evil and transform it through mildness

23. The essential characteristic will be aesthetic pleasure in the good—love of the moral

24. Immoral intellect will deteriorate into animal-humans leading to the 8th Sphere

25. Spirit-Self draws further into moral human beings

26. 6th Epoch can be found in the Astral World, 7th Epoch in the Heavenly World

27. Develop *Faith* in the astral body in the 5th Post-Atlantean Period, *Love* in the etheric body (6th Post-Atlantean Period), *Hope* in the physical body (7th Post-Atlantean Period)

28. Christ appears in the etheric in the 5th Post-Atlantean Period, Christ in the astral in the 6th Post-Atlantean Period, Christ as the group soul of humanity in the 7th Post-Atlantean Period

29. Downfall of our 5th Post-Atlantean Period will be lack of morality and overwhelming evil egotism

30. 5th Post-Atlantean Periods will be destroyed by the War of All against All through evil

31. After the War of All against All, there will be two streams in humanity—good and evil

32. Humans destroy each other except for a tiny handful who survive to 6th Post-Atlantean Period through selflessness

33. After the War of All against All the evil stream will be led to virtue by the good stream and their leader Mani

34. Re-union of the Moon with the Earth

35. Whole Earth-globe will be a self-functioning electric mass ruled by Ahriman

36. A re-union with the Moon in (8,000 AD), and later the re-union of the Earth-Moon with the Sun

37. Earth and humans will then change into an astral heavenly body called by Rudolf Steiner Future Jupiter

38. Love will be able to dissolve matter and build the Future Jupiter globe

39. In the 5th Post-Atlantean Epoch, Christ comes in an etheric body, in the 6th Epoch in an astral body, and in the 7th Epoch in a mighty Cosmic Ego that is the Group-Soul of Humanity

Rudolf Steiner on the 15,120 Year-long Sixth Epoch

The following lectures of Rudolf Steiner concerning the Sixth Epoch (7,894 AD) are perhaps the clearest presentations of this future stage of human development. We can set our sights on these goals and attempt to emulate the type of hybrid human-Angel that is being described here as a type of new icon; that is, so to speak, the metamorphosing of the human "chrysalis" turning into an "Angelic winged butterfly" that longs to fly to its home the Sun.

We have summarized in short statements the main points and descriptions of the Sixth Epoch. To be clear, this is not referring to the 6th Post-Atlantean Period (2,160-year Russian/Slavic Sub-Epoch) that will immediately follow our current 5th Post-Atlantean Period (Anglo-Germanic Sub-Epoch). The Sixth Epoch (15,120 years) presented below comes after the War of All against All. There will still be two Epochs to complete before humans will, in general, have the opportunity to evolve into human-Angels who are clothing themselves with the beings and forces of the Angelic Spirit-Self over these two Epochs. These "predictions" can become the visualization that an aspirant can use to "build their hut in the spiritual world" in the Future Jupiter incarnation of the Earth when humans become Angels in the New Jerusalem of *Revelation*.

Please note the confusion various translators create by the inconsistent use of terms like epochs, ages, epochs of culture, ages of civilizations, post-Atlantean cultures and epochs and so forth. It is often hard to keep track of the various terms, including the Theosophical terms of Races, Root Races, Globes, Rounds, etc. We have tried to provide charts, lists, and diagrams to help resolve those questions for the reader.

Preparing for the Sixth Epoch, Rudolf Steiner, Lecture XIII, 1915, GA 159

"The whole purpose of Spiritual Science is to prepare in this sense for the sixth epoch of culture. Herein we prepare what Spiritual Science calls freedom of thought. By coming together in friendly associations for the purpose of cultivating Spiritual Science, we prepare the culture, the civilization of the sixth post-Atlantean epoch.

In the Sixth Epoch:

- the most highly cultured will not only feel pain such as is caused today by the sight of poverty, suffering and misery in the world, but such individuals will experience the suffering of another human being as their own suffering.

- the well-being of the individual will depend entirely upon the well-being of the whole.

- complete freedom of thought and a longing for it will so lay hold of men that what a man likes to believe, what religious convictions he holds, will rest wholly within the power of his own individuality. Everyone will feel that complete freedom of thought in the domain of religion is a fundamental right of the human being.

- people will only be considered to have real knowledge when they recognize the spiritual, when they know that the spiritual pervades the world and that human souls must unite with the spiritual.

- all materialistic beliefs in science will be regarded as antiquated superstition. Men as a matter of course will accept as science only such forms of knowledge as are based upon the spiritual, upon pneumatology.

- it is the Spirit-Self that must be developed within the souls of men, just as now the Consciousness Soul is being developed. The nature of Spirit-Self is that it must pre-suppose the existence in human souls of the three characteristics of which I have spoken: social life in which brotherliness prevails, freedom of thought, and pneumatology.

- the individual should make preparations for communities into which he will enter entirely of his own free will in the sixth epoch. There hovers before us as a high ideal a form of community that will so encompass the sixth epoch of culture that civilized human beings will quite naturally meet each other as brothers and sisters.

- Eastern Europe will have to wait until the Spirit-Self comes down to the Earth and can permeate the souls of men.

- the Russian soul feels that Spirit-Self is to descend, but that it can only descend into a community of men permeated with the consciousness of brotherhood.

- the spirit of community is needed to bring about the descent of Spirit-Self.

- our aim is to call together human beings who resolve to be brothers and sisters, and above whom hovers something that they strive to develop by cultivating Spiritual Science, feeling the good spirit of brotherhood hovering over and above them.

- we seek for community above us, the living Christ in us."

Challenge of the Times, Lecture V, *Specters of the Old Testament in the Nationalism of the Present*, Rudolf Steiner, December 7, 1918, GA 186

"This is the special mission of Christ in the Fifth Post-Atlantean Epoch—to be the Healer, the One who heals. The other forms of the Christ-Impulse must remain in the background. For the Sixth Post-Atlantean Epoch, the Christ-Impulse must work in the direction of seership. There the Spirit-Self comes to

development within which man cannot live without seership. In the Seventh
Post-Atlantean Epoch a sort of prophetic nature will develop as the third
element, since it must, indeed, pass prophetically over into an entirely new
Period."

Faith, Love, and Hope: Towards the Sixth Epoch, Rudolf Steiner, December 3, 1911, GA 130

"It is a feature of present-day man that he has something in his soul which
is, as it were, a reflection of the nature of faith of the astral body. In the Sixth
Post-Atlantean Epoch there will be a reflection within man of the love-nature
of the etheric body, and in the seventh, before the great catastrophe, the
reflection of the nature of hope of the physical body.

Our age will be followed by one in which the need for love will cast its light.
Love in the Sixth Culture-Epoch will show itself in a very different form—
different even from that which can be called Christian love. Slowly we draw
nearer to that epoch; and by making those in the Anthroposophical Movement
familiar with the mysteries of the Cosmos, with the nature of the various
individualities both on the physical plane and on the higher planes, we try to
kindle love for everything in existence. This is not done so much by talking of
love, as by feeling that what is able to kindle love in the soul is prepared for the
Sixth Epoch by Anthroposophy. Through Anthroposophy the forces of love are
specially aroused in the whole human soul, and that is prepared which a man
needs for gradually acquiring a true understanding of the Mystery of Golgotha.
For it is indeed true that the Mystery of Golgotha came to pass; and the Gospels
have evoked something which yesterday was likened to how children learn to
speak. But the deepest lesson—the mission of Earthly love in its connection
with the Mystery of Golgotha—has not yet been grasped. Full understanding
of this will be possible only in the Sixth Post-Atlantean Culture-Epoch, when
people grow to realize more and more that the foundations for it are actually
within them, and out of their innermost being—in other words, out of love—
do what should be done. When forces wake in our souls which impel us to
do what we should through love alone, we then discover in us something that
must gradually become widespread in the Sixth Culture-Epoch. Then in a man's
nature quite special forces of the etheric body will make themselves known.

There have been, and will continue to be, frequent incorporations of the individuality who appeared as Jeshu ben Pandira, until he rises from the rank of Bodhisattva to that of Buddha. According to our reckoning of time this will be in about 3,000 years. At the same time the teaching will contain—to an extent far greater than it is possible to conceive today—a magical moral force carrying to hearts and souls a full conviction of the eternal, deeply significant brotherhood of intellect and morality.

Maitreya Buddha's task will be to enlighten human beings concerning the Mystery of Golgotha, and for this he will draw ideas and words of the deepest significance from the very language he will use. His words will imprint into men's souls directly, magically, the nature of the Mystery of Golgotha. Hence in this connection also we are approaching what we may call the future moral age of man; in a certain sense we could designate it as a coming Golden Age.

The Christ will gradually reveal Himself to ever-higher powers in human beings, and how the teachers, who up to now have taught only individual peoples and individual men, will become the interpreters of the great Christ-event for all who are willing to listen. And we can point out how, through the dawning of the age of love, conditions for the age of morality are prepared.

Then will come the last Epoch [Seventh Epoch], during which human souls will receive the reflection of what we call hope; when, strengthened through the force flowing from the Mystery of Golgotha and from the age of morality, men will take into themselves forces of hope. This is the most important gift they need in order to face the next catastrophe and to begin a new life."

The Apocalypse of St. John, Rudolf Steiner, June 26, 1908, Nuremberg, GA 104

"And if we follow this path, we shall bring into the sixth age the true spiritual life of wisdom and of love. The spiritual wisdom we have acquired will become the impulse of love in the Sixth Age, which is represented by the community expressing itself even in its name, the community of brotherly love, or Philadelphia. All these names are carefully chosen. Man will develop his "I" to the necessary height, so that he will become independent and in freedom show love towards all other beings in the sixth age, which is represented by the community at Philadelphia. In this way the spiritual life of the sixth age will be prepared. We shall then have found the individual "I" within us to a higher degree, so that no external power can any longer play upon us if we do not wish it; so that we can close and no one without our will can open, and if we open no opposing power can close. These are the Keys of David. For this reason, he who inspires the letter says that he has the Keys of David: "And to the Angel of the community in Philadelphia write: These things saith he that is holy, he that is true, he that hath the key of David, he that openeth, and no man shutteth; and shutteth and no man openeth. Behold, I have set before thee an open door, and no man can shut it (*Revelation* 3:7)—the "I" that has found itself within itself."

In the Seventh Age those who have found this spiritual life will flock around the great Leader; it will unite them around this great Leader. They will already belong so far to the spiritual life that they will be distinguished from those who have fallen away, who are lukewarm, "neither cold nor hot." The little flock which has found spirituality will understand him who may then say, when he makes himself known, "I am he who contains in himself the true final Being towards which everything is steering." For this final Being is described by the word, Amen. "And unto the Angel of the church of Laodicea write: Thus saith the Amen, he who in his being presents the nature of the end." (*Revelation* 3:14)

Significant Facts Pertaining to the Spiritual Life of the Middle of the 19th Century, Rudolf Steiner, Dornach, October 31-November 7, 1915, GA 254

"We are now living in the fifth epoch of the Post-Atlantean Age; then we come into the Sixth and Seventh Epochs. During the Sixth and Seventh Epochs, the rigidity of the etheric body will have a great influence upon the physical body and the physical body will become a faithful copy of the etheric. But these things will have no meaning whatever during the Sixth Epoch, our bodily form will then obtain its expression from the series of our incarnations. The human beings will differ very much from one another, and their features will be strongly marked. When we encounter somebody, we shall then know exactly: This is a good person and that is an evil one. The human countenance will thus more and more express the moral qualities.

During the Sixth Epoch, even the outward physiognomy of our environment will have a very changed aspect. Particularly those animals which now supply meat for human consumption, shall then have died out. In the future, a great hymn of praise will be Sung to vegetarianism, and people will tell one another, as if they were speaking of some ancient memory, that their ancestors used to eat meat. Not all the animals shall then have died out, but only certain species; particularly those animals shall have disappeared from the Earth that have taken on the most rigid forms. Thus, even the Earth and its outward physiognomy will undergo certain changes.

In the future we shall be so firmly bound to a rigid physiognomy, that it will constitute an almost fatal destiny, a real fate, which will be impressed upon our whole being. Moral qualities will be written upon their countenances, upon the physiognomy of their bodies.

Let us bear in mind the fact that if our etheric body is to be strong, so that it may be able to correct the mistakes of our physical body, its strength should be evident through the fact that we learn to consider the things which come to us from the etheric world as something very earnest and real. This will be the attitude which will be able to exercise a more and more healing influence. It will be necessary above all that we should take up Spiritual Science, so as to be prepared for the moment when the etheric shape of Christ shall appear to us, and so that we may take this up with due earnestness and in the right spirit.

We face a time in which we shall first of all discover the Christ, and in His following we shall gradually discover the etheric. Even then, this etheric element will have the strength to make of us individual human beings."

Apocalypse of John, Lecture IV, Rudolf Steiner, Nuremberg, June 1908, GA 104

"This will no longer be the case in the epoch following the great War of All against All. Upon the forehead and in the whole physiognomy it will be written whether the person is good or evil. He will show in his face what is contained in his inmost soul. What a man has developed within himself, whether he has exercised good or evil impulses, will be written on his forehead. After the great War of All against All there will be two kinds of human beings. Those who had previously tried to follow the call to the spiritual life, who cultivated the spiritualizing and ennobling of their inner spiritual life, will show this inward life on their faces and express it in their gestures and the movements of their hands. And those who have turned away from the spiritual life, represented by the community of Laodicea, who were lukewarm, neither warm nor cold, will pass into the following epoch as those who retard human evolution, who preserve the backward forces of evolution which have been left behind. They will show the evil passions, impulses, and instincts hostile to the spiritual in an ugly, unintelligent, evil-looking countenance. In their gestures and hand-movements, in everything they do, they will present an outer image of the ugliness in their soul. Just as humanity has separated into races and communities, in the future it will divide into two great streams, the good and the evil. And what is in their souls will be outwardly manifest, they will no longer be able to hide it."

The Manicheans, Rudolf Steiner, Berlin, November 11, 1904, GA 93

"Mani will prepare for that epoch in which the men of the Sixth Root Race will be led by themselves, by the light of their own souls. Mani will create an overlapping stream, a stream which goes further than the stream of the Rosicrucians. The stream of Mani goes over to the Sixth Root Race which has been in preparation since the founding of Christianity. Christianity will appear in its perfected form in the Sixth Root Race.

A number of human beings must be formed into an organization, a form, in which the Christianity of the Sixth Root Race can find its place. In this Sixth Root Race, good and evil will form a far greater contrast than they do today. In the Sixth Root Race, evil will appear, especially in the spiritual. There will be men who are mighty in love and goodness. But evil will also be there as a mood and a disposition without any covering within a large number of human beings. They will extol evil. The task of the Sixth Root Race is to draw evil again into itself through gentleness. It must express itself in the forming of a community which has to spread above all things: peace, love, and non-resistance to evil."

Gospel of John, Lecture X, Rudolf Steiner, Hamburg, May 30, 1908, GA 103

"Just think how orderly the plants grow; each plant grows toward the Sun and there is only a single Sun. When in the same way, in the course of the Sixth Cultural Epoch, that Spirit-Self draws into human beings, a Spiritual Sun will actually be present, toward which all men will incline, and in which they will become harmonized. That is the great perspective which we have in prospect for the sixth epoch.

But we now see clearly that an epoch will come, the Sixth, which will be a very important one; important, because it will bring Peace and Brotherhood through a common Wisdom. Peace and Brotherhood, because not only will the Higher Self sink down into its lower form as Spirit-Self or Manas in certain chosen human beings, but also in that part of humanity passing through a normal evolution. A union of the human ego, as it has been gradually evolved with the higher, the unifying Ego, will then take place. We may call this a spiritual marriage and the union of the human ego with Manas or Spirit-Self was always so called in Esoteric Christianity. What is to happen to mankind in the Sixth Epoch must be slowly and gradually prepared. The power and force of what is to take place within mankind in the Sixth Epoch has to come from without."

The Seven Trumpets
7th Post-Atlantean
Period

The 7th Post-Atlantean Period (Sub-Epoch) is referred to in *Revelation* as the Church of Laodicea. Rudolf Steiner tells us that it is the virtue of hope that must be developed to meet the challenges of this Period. The quality of lukewarmness will be shunned as if it too were part of the evil race that will stand against the good race of people who have united with the great teacher to usher in a new age of Christianity that was developed in the 6th Post-Atlantean Period. Steiner also tells us that the Angels of the seven trumpets unleash the forces that lead ultimately to the War of All against All. The author of *Revelation* describes the seven stages of the 7th Post-Atlantean Period in the following manner:

1. *The First Angel* "And when he had opened the seventh seal, there was silence in heaven about the space of half an hour. And I saw the seven angels which stood before God; and to them were given seven trumpets. And another angel came and stood at the altar, having a golden censer; and there was given unto him much incense, that he should offer it with the prayers of all saints upon the golden altar which was before the throne. And the smoke of the incense, which came with the prayers of the saints, ascended up before God out of the angel's hand. And the angel took the censer, and filled it with fire of the altar, and cast it into the earth: and there were voices, and thunderings, and lightnings, and an earthquake. And the seven angels which had the seven trumpets prepared themselves to sound. The first angel sounded, and there followed hail and fire mingled with blood, and they were cast upon the earth: and the third part of trees was burnt up, and all green grass was burnt up." (*Revelation* 8:7)

2. "*The Second Angel* sounded his trumpet, and something like a huge mountain, all ablaze, was thrown into the sea. A third of the sea turned into blood, a third

of the living creatures in the sea died, and a third of the ships were destroyed." (*Revelation* 8:8-9)

3. "*The Third Angel* sounded his trumpet, and a great star, blazing like a torch, fell from the sky on a third of the rivers and on the springs of water—the name of the star is Wormwood. A third of the waters turned bitter, and many people died from the waters that had become bitter." (*Revelation* 8:10-11)

4. "*The Fourth Angel* sounded his trumpet, and a third of the Sun was struck, a third of the Moon, and a third of the stars, so that a third of them turned dark. A third of the day was without light, and also a third of the night." (*Revelation* 8:12)

5. "*The Fifth Angel* sounded his trumpet, and I saw a star that had fallen from the sky to the Earth. The star was given the key to the shaft of the Abyss. When he opened the Abyss, smoke rose from it like the smoke from a gigantic furnace. The Sun and sky were darkened by the smoke from the Abyss. And out of the smoke locusts came down on the Earth and were given power like that of scorpions of the Earth. They were told not to harm the grass of the Earth or any plant or tree, but only those people who did not have the seal of God on their foreheads. They were not allowed to kill them but only to torture them for five months. And the agony they suffered was like that of the sting of a scorpion when it strikes. During those days people will seek death but will not find it; they will long to die, but death will elude them. The locusts looked like horses prepared for battle. On their heads they wore something like crowns of gold, and their faces resembled human faces." (*Revelation* 9:1-12)

6. "*The Sixth Angel* sounded his trumpet, and I heard a voice coming from the four horns of the golden altar that is before God. It said to the sixth Angel who had the trumpet, 'Release the four Angels who are bound at the great river Euphrates.' And the four Angels who had been kept ready for this very hour and day and month and year were released to kill a third of mankind. The number of the mounted troops was twice ten thousand times ten thousand. I heard their number. The horses and riders I saw in my vision looked like this: Their breastplates were fiery red, dark blue, and yellow as sulfur. The heads of the horses resembled the heads of lions, and out of their mouths came fire, smoke and sulfur. A third of mankind was killed by the three plagues of fire, smoke and sulfur that came out of their mouths. The power of the horses was in their mouths and in their tails; for their tails were like snakes, having heads with which they inflict injury. The rest of mankind who were not killed by these plagues still

did not repent of the work of their hands; they did not stop worshiping demons, and idols of gold, silver, bronze, stone and wood-idols that cannot see or hear or walk. Nor did they repent of their murders, their magic arts, their sexual immorality or their thefts." (*Revelation* 9:13-21)

7. "*The Seventh Angel* sounded his trumpet, and there were loud voices in heaven, which said: 'The kingdom of the world has become the kingdom of our Lord and of his Messiah, and he will reign for ever and ever.'" (*Revelation* 11:15)

Rudolf Steiner Concerning the American 7th Period

Apocalypse of John, Lecture VIII, Rudolf Steiner, Nuremberg, June 25, 1908, GA 104

"Our Fifth Post-Atlantean Epoch will end, when the seventh age [Seventh Post-Atlantean Period (Sub-Epoch)] has passed away, by the War of All against All. It has become clear to us that this "I" of man has developed from a group-soul nature, from a kind of all-inclusive universal "I" out of which it has been differentiated. It would be wrong if man were to crave to go down again with his "I" into some sort of universal consciousness, into some sort of common consciousness. Everything which causes a man to strive to lose his "I" and dissolve it into a universal consciousness, is the result of weakness. He alone understands the "I" who knows that after he has gained it in the course of cosmic evolution it cannot be lost; and above all man must strive for the strength to make this "I" more and more inward, more and more divine.

Thus the "I" will be the pledge for the highest goal of man. But at the same time, if it does not discover love, if it hardens within itself, it is the tempter that plunges him into the Abyss. For it is that which separates men from one another which brings them to the great War of All against All, not only to the war of nation against nation but to the war of each single person against every other person in every branch of life; to the war of class against class, of caste against caste, and sex against sex. Thus, in every field of life the "I" will become the apple of discord; and hence we may say that it can lead on the one hand to the highest and on the other hand to the lowest. For this reason, it is a sharp two-edged sword.

From the Sixth Age [Sixth Post-Atlantean Period (Sub-Epoch)] will be taken those human souls who have to pass over into the following [Sixth] Epoch. After the War of All against All, there will be expressed in the features all that is in our age being prepared in men's souls. The so-called Seventh Age [including Seventh Post-Atlantean Period (Sub-Epoch)] will be of very little importance. We are now living in the 5th [Post-Atlantean Period (Sub-Epoch)] Age of Civilization; then follows the 6th [Post-Atlantean Period (Sub-Epoch)], from which will proceed a number of people full of understanding for the spiritual world, filled with the spirit of brotherly love, which results from spiritual knowledge. The ripest fruit of our present civilization will appear in the 6th [Post-Atlantean Period (Sub-Epoch)] Age. And that which follows it will be what is lukewarm, neither warm nor cold; the 7th [Post-Atlantean Period (Sub-Epoch)] Age is something like an overripe fruit, which outlasts the War of All against All, but contains no principle of progress.

We are now looking with great longing towards the Sixth Civilization [Sixth Post-Atlantean Epoch], to that which must be described as developing out of the spiritual marriage between West and East. The Sixth stage will be the foundation for the new civilizations which will arise after the great War of All against All; just as our civilization arose after the Atlantean Epoch. On the other hand, the Seventh race of culture [Seventh Post-Atlantean Period (Sub-Epoch)] will be characterized by the lukewarm. This Seventh Age will continue into the new Epoch, just as the Sixth and Seventh races of the Atlantean Epoch continued into our Epoch as races were hardened and stiffening. After the War of All against All, there will be two streams in humanity: on the one hand the stream of Philadelphia will survive with the principle of progress, of inner freedom, of brotherly love, a small group drawn from every tribe and nation; and on the other hand, the great mass of all those who are lukewarm, the remains of those who are now becoming lukewarm (Laodicea).

After the great War of All against All, gradually the evil stream will be led over to good by the good race, by the good stream. This will be one of the principal tasks after the great War of All against All; to rescue what can be rescued from those who after the great war will only have the impulse to fight one another and to allow the "I" to express itself in the most external egoism. Such things are always provided for in advance in the spiritual guidance of humanity.

Do not consider it a hard thing in the plan of creation, as something which should be altered, that humanity will be divided into those who will stand on the right and those who will stand on the left; consider it rather as something that is wise in the highest degree in the plan of creation. Consider that through the evil separating from the good, the good will receive its greatest strengthening. For after the great War of All against All, the good will have to make every possible effort to rescue the evil during the period in which this will still be possible. For in this next great Epoch men will understand how to set occult forces in motion. The good will have the task of working upon their brothers of the evil movement.

Everything is prepared beforehand in the hidden occult movements; but the deepest of all occult cosmic currents is the least understood. The most capable must be chosen and prepared to live beyond the period of the great War of All against All when men will confront those who bear in their countenances the sign of evil; they must be so prepared that as much good force as possible will flow into humanity. It will still be possible for those bodies, which are to a certain extent soft, to be transformed after the War of All against All by the converted souls, by the souls who will still be led to the good in this last Epoch. In this way much will be accomplished. The good would not be so great a good if it were not to grow through the conquest of evil. Love would not be so intense if it had not to become love so great as to be able even to overcome the wickedness in the countenances of evil men. Those who are being prepared in their souls by such teachings, so that in the future they will, be able to accomplish this great task of education, are the pupils of the Manichaean School. Manes [Mani] is that exalted individuality, who is repeatedly incarnated on the Earth, who is the guiding spirit of those whose task it is to transform evil.

For if we have had to say that already in the Sixth Epoch men will show good and evil on their faces, we shall have to say all the more of the Seventh that the form of man and the forms of all the other beings will be an expression of good and evil to a much higher degree than in the Sixth Epoch. All matter will bear the stamp of the spirit. There will be absolutely nothing in this Seventh Epoch that can be hidden in any way. Even those belonging to the Sixth Epoch will be unable to hide anything from him who has the necessary vision. An evil man will express his evil, a good man

will express the good that is within him; but in the Seventh Epoch it will
be quite impossible by speech to hide what is in the soul. Thought will no
longer remain dumb so that it can be hidden, for when the soul thinks, its
thought will ring forth outwardly. It will then be just as thought is already
to the initiates today. To them, thought now rings out in Devachan. But
this Devachan will have descended into the physical world, just as the astral
world will have descended into the physical world in the Sixth Epoch. Even
now the Sixth Epoch can be found in the astral world and the Seventh in the
heavenly world.

The Sixth Epoch is the descended astral world, that is to say the images,
the expressions, the manifestations of it. The Seventh Epoch will be the
descended heavenly world [Devachan], the expression of it. And then the
Earth will have reached the goal of its physical evolution. The Earth, together
with all its beings, will then change into an astral heavenly body. Physical
substance, as such, will disappear. The part which until then had been able to
spiritualize itself, will pass over into the spirit, into astral substance. Imagine
all the beings of the Earth who up to that time have been able to express what
is good, noble, intellectual and beautiful in their external material form; who
will bear an expression of Christ Jesus in their countenances, whose words
will manifest Christ Jesus; for they will ring out as resounding thoughts—all
these will have the power to dissolve what they have within them as physical
matter, as warm water dissolves salt. Everything physical will pass over into
an astral globe. But those who up to that time have not progressed so far as to
be a material and corporeal expression of what is noble, beautiful, intellectual
and good, will not have the power to dissolve matter; for them matter will
remain. They will become hardened in matter; they will retain material form.
At this point in the Earth's evolution there will be an ascent into the Spirit of
Forms which will live in the astral and which will separate from themselves
another material globe, a globe which will contain beings unfit for the ascent
because they are unable to dissolve the material part. In this way our Earth
will advance towards its future. Through the souls gradually refining matter
from within, the substance of the Earth will become more and more refined
until it receives the power to dissolve. Then will come the time when the
insoluble part will be ejected as a special planet. In the course of seven ages
that which has hardened itself in matter will be driven out, and the power

which drives it out will be the opposite force to that which will have forced the good beings upward.

What, then, will they have used to dissolve matter? The power of love gained through the Christ-Principle. Beings become capable of dissolving matter through taking love into their souls. The more the soul is warmed by love the more powerfully will it be able to work on matter; it will spiritualize the whole Earth and transform it into an astral Globe. But just as love dissolves matter, as warm water dissolves salt, so will the opposite of love press down—again throughout seven stages everything which has not become capable of fulfilling the Earth mission. The contrary of divine love is called divine wrath, that is the technical expression for it. Just as in the course of the Fourth Stage of Civilization this love was imprinted in humanity, just as it will become warmer and warmer through the last stages in our Epoch, the Sixth and Seventh, so on the other hand there is growing that which hardens matter around itself—the divine wrath. In the last Epoch, the Epoch of the sounding of the trumpets, you would with spiritual vision see how men consist of delicate, spiritualized bodies; and how those who have hardened the material principle in themselves have preserved in themselves what today are the most important constituents of matter; and how this will fall as husks into the material globe which will be left after the Epoch indicated by the sounding of the trumpets.

Man's outer body will thus become an expression of the good by his receiving the highest message, the highest teaching there is on this Earth; and this highest teaching is the message of Christ Jesus on the Earth. We must take it up thoroughly, not merely with the understanding; we must take it into our innermost being, just as one takes nourishment into the physical body. And as humanity develops further it will take up the joyful message into its inner being more and more. It is just this reception of the message of love which it will have to regard as the result of the Earth's mission."

Reading the Pictures of the Apocalypse, Cosmogony, Rudolf Steiner, Paris, June 14, 1906, GA 104

"After our Fifth Epoch another will come, the Sixth, which will be related to ours as a spiritually minded soul is related to a rationally inclined soul. This

Epoch will bring genius, clairvoyance, the creative spirit, to development. How will Christianity appear in the sixth Epoch? The faithful reverence of the person of Christ, the god of the human being on the Earth, has for a certain time taken the place of occult science and the mysteries. But the two streams will be united in the Sixth Epoch. The mechanical science of the physical plane will be elevated to the heights of spiritual creative power. That will be gnosis or spiritual knowledge. This Sixth Epoch will be radically different from ours. Great, tumultuous catastrophes will precede it, for the Sixth Epoch will be just as spiritual as ours is materialistic; but, such a transformation can only occur through great, physical upheavals. Everything that will be formed in the course of the Sixth Epoch will call into existence the possibility of a Seventh Epoch which itself will form the end of these post-Atlantean Cultures [Epochs] and will know completely different conditions of life from our own. This Seventh Epoch will end with a revolution of the elements, similar to the one that brought an end to the Atlantean continent.

Human beings always carry within themselves what they will see around them in future times. All that presently exists around us actually came forth from us in preceding ages.

What human beings possess today as their inner soul life, their thoughts, their feelings, will similarly be revealed externally and become the environment in which people live. The future resides in the hearts of men and women. The choice is ours to decide for a future of good or of evil. Just as it is true that the human being once left behind something that then became the world of animals, so too, what is evil in the human being will one day form a kind of degenerate humanity. At the present time, we can more or less hide the good or evil within us. A day will come when we can no longer do this, when the good or the evil will be written indelibly on our forehead, on our body, and even on the face of the Earth. Humanity will then be split into two races. In the same way that we encounter boulders or animals today, in the future we will encounter beings of pure evil and ugliness. When a human being's facial features become an expression of that individual's karma, then people will separate themselves according to the stream in which they apparently belong. Everything depends on whether human beings have conquered the lower nature within them or whether this lower nature has triumphed over the spirit."

An Esoteric Cosmology, Lecture XVIII, *The Apocalypse*,
Rudolf Steiner, Paris, 1906, GA 94

"Our Fifth Epoch will be followed by another, the Sixth. This Sixth Epoch will see the development of brotherhood among men, clairvoyance, and creative power. What will Christianity be in the Sixth Epoch? To the priest in the Mysteries before Christ, there was harmony between science and faith. Science and faith were one and the same. When he looked up to the heavens, the priest knew that the soul was a drop of water from the celestial ocean, led down to Earth by the great streams of life flowing through space. Now that the attention of men is wholly directed to the physical world, faith has need of a refuge, of religion. Hence the separation between science and faith. Faith in the Person of Christ, of the God-Man on Earth has temporarily replaced Occult Science and the Mysteries of antiquity. But in the Sixth Epoch, the two streams will again unite. Mechanical science will become spiritually creative. This will be Gnosis-spiritual consciousness. This Sixth Epoch, which will be radically different from our own and will be preceded by mighty cataclysms. It will be as spiritual as ours has been material. But the transformation can only be brought about by physical catastrophes. The Sixth Epoch will prepare for a Seventh Epoch. This Seventh Epoch will be the end of the Post-Atlantean civilizations and conditions of earthly life will be entirely different from those we know. At the end of the Seventh Epoch there will be a revolution of the elements analogous to that which put an end to Atlantis, and the subsequent eras will know a spirituality prepared by the two preceding Post-Atlantean Periods.

Thus, there are seven great periods [Post-Atlantean] of Aryan civilization in which the laws of evolution slowly come to expression. At first, man has within him what he later sees around him. All that is actually around us now, passed out from us in a preceding Epoch when our being was still mingled with the Earth, Moon, and Sun.

All that lives today in the inner being of man, his thoughts, his feelings, will find expression in the outer world and become his surroundings. The future lies within man. He is free to make it good or evil. Just as he has already left the animal kingdom behind him, so the evil in him today will form a race of degenerate beings. In our age, man can to a certain extent hide the good or evil within him. But a time will come when he will no longer be able to do so, when the good and the evil will be written in indelible characters upon his countenance, upon his body, nay even upon the very face of the Earth.

Humanity will then divide into two races. Just as today we see rocks or animals, in that future age we shall encounter beings who are wholly evil, wholly ugly. In our time it is only the clairvoyant who is able to see moral goodness or moral ugliness in human beings. But when man's very features express his karma, human beings will divide into groups of themselves, according to the stream to which they manifestly belong, according to whether the lower nature has been conquered or whether it has conquered the Spirit. This differentiation is beginning to operate little by little. When we derive understanding of the future from the past, and strive to realize the ideal of this future, its plan begins to unfold before us. A new race will come into being to be the link between the man of the present and the spiritual man of the future.

It was taught in Manicheism that from our age onwards the souls of men would begin to transmute into good the evil which will manifest in full force in the Sixth Epoch. In other words: human souls must be strong enough to bring good out of evil by a process of spiritual alchemy.

When the Earth begins to recapitulate the previous phases of its evolution, there will first be a re-union with the Moon, and then of this Earth-Moon with the Sun. The re-union with the Moon will mark the culminating point of evil on the Earth; the re-union with the Sun will signify, on the other hand, the advent of happiness, the reign of the 'elect.' Man will bear the signs of the seven great phases of the Earth. The Book with the Seven Seals, spoken of in the *Apocalypse*, will be opened. The Woman clothed with the Sun who has the Moon under her feet, refers to the age when the Earth will once again be united with Sun and Moon. The Trumpets of Judgment will sound for the Earth and will have passed into the Devachanic condition where the ruling principle is not light but sound. The hallmark of the end of Earthly existence will be that the Christ-Principle permeates all humanity. Having become like unto Christ, men will gather around Him as the hosts around the Lamb, and the great harvest of evolution will constitute the new Jerusalem."

The Work of Secret Societies in the World, The Atom as Coagulated Electricity, Rudolf Steiner, Berlin, December 23, 1904, GA 93

"We are going forward to an age when, as I indicated recently, men will understand what the atom is, in reality. It will be realized—by the public mind too—that the atom is nothing but coagulated electricity and that thought itself is composed of the same substance.

The attainment of selflessness alone will enable humanity to be kept from the brink of destruction. The downfall of our present Epoch will be caused by lack of morality. Our Epoch and its civilization will be destroyed by the War of All against All, by evil. Human beings will destroy each other in mutual strife. A tiny handful of men will make good and thus insure their survival in the Sixth Epoch of Civilization. This tiny handful will have attained selflessness.

In the Seventh Epoch of Civilization, this War of All against All will break out in the most terrible form. Great and mighty forces will be let loose by the discoveries, turning the whole Earth-globe into a kind of self-functioning live electric mass. In a way that cannot be discussed, the tiny handful will be protected and preserved.

Freemasonry was aware of its duty to build an edifice dedicated to selfless ends. It is easier to become one of the tiny handful of men who ensure for themselves a place in the life of the future by using the good old forms than by having to struggle out of chaos. Thus, there are definite stages for the investigation of the secrets of future phases of evolution. The high Degrees of Freemasonry originally had no other aim or purpose than to be an expression, each one of them, of a future stage of the evolution of humanity. Thus, we have in Freemasonry something that has been both good and beautiful. A man who attained one Degree knew how he must work his way into the future; he could be a kind of pioneer. Nation, race, sex, position, religion... all these work upon human egoism. Only when man has overcome them will he be free of egoism."

Buddha and Christ, The Sphere of the Bodhisattvas, Rudolf Steiner, Milan, September 21, 1911, GA 130

"The main characteristic of the Sixth Epoch will be that very definite feelings regarding what is moral and what is immoral will arise in the souls of men.

Delicate feelings of sympathy will be aroused by compassionate, kind deeds and feelings of antipathy by malicious actions. The Sixth Epoch will be followed by the seventh, when the moral life will be still further deepened. Whereas in the Sixth Epoch man will take pleasure in good and noble actions, in the Seventh Epoch the natural outcome of such pleasure will be a moral impulse, that is to say there will be a firm resolve to do what is moral. The essential characteristic of the following Epoch will be aesthetic pleasure in the good, aesthetic displeasure in the evil.

Let us think once again of the phases of evolution through the Fifth, Sixth and Seventh Post-Atlantean Culture Periods in order to grasp how intellectuality, aestheticism, and morality will come to expression in men's life of soul. In the Sixth Epoch, that is, from about the third millennium onwards, immorality will have a paralyzing effect upon intellectuality. The mental powers of a man who is intellectual and at the same time immoral will definitely deteriorate and this condition will become more and more pronounced in the future evolution of humanity. A man who has no morals will therefore have no intellectual power for this will depend entirely upon moral actions; and in the Seventh Epoch, cleverness without morality will be non-existent.

And during the next three thousand years, the number of those able to behold the etheric Christ will steadily increase, until in about three thousand years, reckoning from the present time, there will be a sufficient number of human beings on the Earth who will need no *Gospels* or other such records, because in their own life of soul they will have actual vision of the Christ.

Hence during the next three thousand years men will have to acquire in the physical world the power to behold the supersensible Christ, and it is the mission of the Anthroposophical Movement to create, first of all, the conditions which make understanding of Christ possible on the physical plane, and then the power to behold Him.

The Christ-Individuality was on the Earth in the body of Jesus of Nazareth for three years only and does not come again in a physical body; in the Fifth Post-Atlantean Epoch He comes in an etheric body, in the Sixth Epoch in an astral body, and in the Seventh [Epoch] in a mighty Cosmic Ego that is like a great Group-Soul of Humanity.

We therefore see how starting from a physical man on Earth, the Christ gradually evolves as Etheric Christ, as Astral Christ, as Ego-Christ, in order, as Ego-Christ, to be the Spirit of the Earth who then rises to even higher stages together with all mankind.

The words uttered by the Maitreya Buddha will contain a magic power that will become moral impulses in the men who hear them. The utterances of the Maitreya Buddha will be permeated in a miraculous way with the power of Christ."

Foundations of Esotericism, Rudolf Steiner, Lecture 25, Berlin, October 27, 1905, GA 93

"In the Seventh Round [Epoch] man will create himself. He will then be able to duplicate, to reproduce himself. In the Seventh Round [Epoch] everyone will have reached the stage at which our Masters stand today. Then our ego will be the bearer of all Earthly experiences. To begin with this will be concentrated in the Lodge of the Masters. The higher ego then will draw itself together, become atomic and form the atoms of Future Jupiter.

The White Lodge will be looked upon as a unity, an ego comprising everything. All human egos and all separateness will be given up and will flow together into the all-comprehensive universal consciousness; great circles, expanded from within, each having a special color, all assembled together in one single circle. When one thinks of them as laid one upon the other, the result is an all-inclusive color. All the egos are within it, making a whole. This immense globe, contracted, constitutes the atom. This multiplies itself, creating itself out of itself. These then are the atoms which will form Future Jupiter. The Moon Adepts formed the atoms of the present-day Earth. One can study the atom when one studies the plan of the Adepts Lodge on the Moon.

On the future Venus a complete consciousness in the etheric body will develop. Then, while man sleeps, he will gain a consciousness concerning the other side of the world. On Future Vulcan the spirit is completely detached; he has then taken the etheric body also with him. This condition endows man with an exact knowledge of the entire world."

Theosophy of the Rosicrucians, Rudolf Steiner, Lecture 8, GA 99

"That the human being can pass through seven such planetary conditions is the meaning of evolution. Each planetary stage is bound up with the development of one of the seven states of human consciousness, and through what takes place on each planet the physical organs for such a state of consciousness are perfected. You will have a more highly developed organ, a psychic organ, on Future Jupiter; on Future Venus there will be an organ through which man will be able to develop physically the consciousness possessed by the initiate today on the Devachanic plane. And on Future Vulcan, the spiritual consciousness will prevail which the initiate possesses today when he is in Higher Devachan, the World of Reason.

So inconceivably much has gone into our becoming what we are. And there is so inconceivably much contained in the Earth evolution that is still to come, and in our passage through the spheres of Future Jupiter, Future Venus, and Future Vulcan. Only little by little does one disentangle oneself from the implications of current thought and approach that which, because it is more spiritual, is more difficult to conceive and is rarely touched on by the habitual thinking of people of today. Observing man as he presently is on Earth, we see that the seeds, so to speak, of what will develop during Future Jupiter, Future Venus, and Future Vulcan already are hidden within him. But the human being is also the result of the Old Saturn, Old Sun, and Old Moon spheres. Yesterday I said that wisdom and everything concerned with truth was established on Old Sun and will be completed on Future Jupiter. The seed that was planted on Old Sun will, more or less, complete its development on Future Jupiter. Thus, we can say: The period within which truth develops stretches from Old Sun to Future Jupiter. On Future Jupiter truth will have become thoroughly inward, and so will have become wisdom: Truth becomes wisdom."

Occult Science, Rudolf Steiner, *The Present and Future of Cosmic Evolution*, GA 13

"The transformations in the things of the Earth existing outside the human being occur with a certain relationship to humanity's own evolution. After the Seventh Cultural Period has run its course, the Earth will be visited by a catastrophe that may be likened to what occurred between the Atlantean and Post-Atlantean Ages [Epochs], and the transformed Earth conditions after this catastrophe will again evolve in seven time periods. Human souls who will then be incarnated will experience, at a higher stage, the union with the higher world experienced by the Atlanteans at a lower stage. Only those human beings, however, in whom are incarnated souls that have developed in a manner possible through the influences of the Greco-Latin Cultural Period and the subsequent Fifth, Sixth, and Seventh Cultural Periods of the Post-Atlantean evolution will be able to cope with the newly formed Earth conditions. The inner being of such souls will correspond to what the Earth has then become. Other souls will then have to remain behind, whereas previously they would have had the choice of creating the conditions for advancement. Souls who will have created the possibility for themselves, in the transition from the Fifth to the Sixth Post-Atlantean Period of penetrating supersensible knowledge with the forces of intellect and feeling, will have the maturity for the corresponding conditions following the next great catastrophe. The Fifth and Sixth Periods are, so to speak, decisive. In the Seventh, the souls who will have reached the goal of the Sixth will develop correspondingly further; the other souls, however, will, under the changed conditions of the environment, find but little opportunity of retrieving what they have neglected. Only at some future time will conditions appear again that will permit this. Evolution thus advances from age to age.

Supersensible cognition not only observes such future changes in which the Earth alone takes part, but it is also aware of changes that occur in co-operation with the heavenly bodies in its environment. A time will come when the evolution of the Earth and mankind will have advanced so far that the spiritual powers and beings that had to sever themselves from the Earth during the Lemurian Age, in order to make possible the continued progress of the Earth's beings, will be able to unite themselves again with the Earth. The Moon will then reunite with the Earth. This will occur because at that time a sufficiently large number of human souls will possess so much inner strength that they will use these Moon forces for the benefit of further evolution. This will occur at a time when, alongside the high level of development that will have been reached by a certain number of human souls, another development will occur that has taken the direction toward evil. The laggard souls will have accumulated in their karma so much error, ugliness, and evil that they will form, for the time being, a special union of evil and aberrant human beings who violently oppose the community of good men.

The good humanity will through its development acquire the use of the Moon forces and thereby transform the evil part also that, as a special realm of the Earth, it may participate in further evolution. Through this work of the good humanity, the Earth, united with the Moon, will be able, after a certain period of evolution, to reunite also with the Sun and with the other planets. Then, after an intermediate stage, which presents itself as a sojourn in a higher world, the Earth will transform itself into [Future] Jupiter. Within this state, what is now called the mineral kingdom will no longer exist; the forces of this mineral kingdom will be transformed into plant forces. The plant kingdom, which in contrast to the present plant kingdom will have an entirely new form, appears during the [Future] Jupiter state as the lowest kingdom. To this a higher kingdom is added, the transformed animal kingdom; above it there is a human kingdom, which proves to be the progeny of the evil community that arose on the Earth; above all these are to be found the descendants of the good community of Earth men, a human kingdom of a higher order. A great part of the activity of this latter human kingdom consists in the work of ennobling the fallen souls of the evil community, so that they may still be able to find their way back into the actual human kingdom.

The [Future] Venus evolution will be one in which the plant kingdom also will have disappeared; the lowest kingdom at that time will be the retransformed animal kingdom; this will be joined on an ascending scale by three human kingdoms of different degrees of perfection. During the [Future] Venus state the Earth remains united with the Sun; during the [Future] Jupiter state, however, evolution proceeds in such a way that at a certain point of time the Sun departs once more from [Future] Jupiter and the latter receives its effects from the outside. After a time, the union of the Sun and [Future] Jupiter ([Future] Jupiter minus the Sun in contradistinction to Jupiter with the Sun) again occurs and the transformation gradually proceeds over into the [Future] Venus state. During that state a special cosmic body splits off that contains all the beings who have resisted evolution, a so to speak "irredeemable Moon," which now moves toward an evolution, for the character of which no expression can be found because it is too dissimilar to anything that man can experience on Earth. The evolved mankind, however, advances in a completely spiritualized existence to the [Future] Vulcan evolution, the description of which does not lie within the scope of this book."

Mystery Centers, Rudolf Steiner, Lecture 9, GA 232

"And now when the pupil felt everything flowing together into his heart which he had experienced earlier, all that he had experienced in his soul manifested itself at the same time as the experience of the planet. Man has a thought. The thought does not remain within the skin of the man. The thought begins to resound. The thought becomes Word. That which the man lives, forms itself into Word. In the Future Vulcan-planet the Word spreads itself out. Everything in the Future Vulcan-planet is speaking, living Being. Word sounds to Word. Word explains itself by Word. Word speaks to Word. Word learns to understand Word. Man feels himself as the World-understanding Word, as the Word-world understanding Word. While this was present before the candidate for Initiation in Hibernia, he knew himself to be in the Future Vulcan existence, in the last metamorphosed condition of the Earth-planet."

Superhuman Helpers from Mercury, Venus, and Vulcan

Rudolf Steiner's reference to "Supermen [Superhuman beings] from Venus, Mercury, and Vulcan" who are here in our time inspiring humanity" creates a question that is quite profound and needs to be understood if we wish to encounter the beings who have helped create and inspire Spiritual Science.

The question of superhuman helpers of humanity is written about and yet little is understood concerning what Dr. Steiner has said about this topic. It is often debated whether these beings are forms of the Angels, Archangels, and Archai who are intimately connected to human development through thinking, feeling, and willing; or are these beings aspects of our own threefold spirit that manifest through the forces of Imagination, Inspiration, and Intuition. Some people have even argued that these beings are, in fact, the higher nature of humanity from the future coming to us to bring the three spiritual principles of the Spirit-Self, Life-Spirit, and Spirit-Man [Spirit Human] into the souls of humans.

Much could be said about these different opinions and thus, the debate continues. Personally, I take up the side of the debate that these are higher hierarchical beings, since in one place Steiner refers to "other beings—not of the human order", and in another place calls them "heavenly beings." Unfortunately, these indications are not definitive and leave plenty of wiggle-room for further discussion. These quotes are also confounded by the fact that Steiner has also referred to our "older brothers and sisters from the Pleiades" who are working together with human beings for the advancement of Spiritual Science and human spiritual development.

References to 'supermen from Vulcan' and 'older brothers and sisters from the Pleiades' stir the imagination and bring many unanswered questions to mind. But the bottom line seems clear in that the "ever present help of the spiritual world" is always there to support humans in taking the next step in wedding their soul to their spirit. The being Anthroposophia is called the 'mid-wife of the soul helping birth the spirit' who 'passes through' the human being whenever another step is taken towards the spirit. So, whether it is Anthroposophia, the Archangel Michael, our Guardian Angel, one or another of the nine hierarchical ranks of spiritual beings, the Holy Trinity, supermen from Venus/Mercury/Vulcan, our higher self, or siblings from the Pleiades doesn't seem to matter so much if we know that our efforts toward the spirit will be aided by spiritual beings anxious for our evolution.

We present below a few selections of Rudolf Steiner's indications concerning the future 'Incarnations of the Earth' called Future Jupiter, Future Venus, and Future Vulcan and the beings associated with those future stages of human spiritual development. These stages align with humans evolving into Angels, Archangels, and Archai in the distant future. But since time and space will transform radically as these stages of development unfold, we could rightly ask the question: "Are these spiritual beings who are here to help us actually our three higher spiritual selves coming to wed our soul to the spirit?" This question, and many others concerning these indications are yet to be fully answered and understood. Only time will tell if our spirit is working with hierarchical beings to aid in our personal spiritual development, or that our own three higher selves are helping our personal evolution from the future, or if our world is populated by spiritual beings who wish to help us evolve. We hope that the selections below will help you formulate your own opinions concerning these transcendent questions and aid in developing Spiritual Science within your soul and spirit.

Rudolf Steiner on Superhuman Helpers

Materialism and the Task of Anthroposophy, Rudolf Steiner, Lecture 14, GA 204

"Thus, since the eighties of the nineteenth century, heavenly beings are seeking to enter this Earth existence. Just as the Vulcan beings were the last to come down to Earth, so Vulcan beings are now actually entering this Earth existence. Heavenly beings are already here in our Earth existence. And it is thanks to the fact that beings from beyond the Earth are bringing messages down into this Earthly existence that it is possible at all to have a comprehensive Spiritual Science today.

Taken as a whole, however, how does the human race behave? If I may say so, the human race behaves in a cosmically rude way toward the beings who are appearing from the Cosmos on Earth, albeit, to begin with, only slowly. Humanity takes no notice of them, ignores them. It is this that will lead the Earth into increasingly tragic conditions. For, in the course of the next few centuries, more and more spirit beings will move among us whose language we ought to understand. We shall understand it only if we seek to comprehend what comes from them, namely, the contents of Spiritual Science. This is what they wish to bestow on us. They want us to act according to Spiritual Science; they want this Spiritual Science to be translated into social action and the conduct of earthly life.

Since the last third of the nineteenth century, we are actually dealing with the influx of spirit beings from the universe. Initially, these were beings dwelling in the sphere between the Moon and Mercury; but they are closing in upon Earth, so to say, seeking to gain a foothold in earthly life through human beings imbuing themselves with thoughts of spiritual beings in the Cosmos. This is another way of describing what I outlined earlier when I said that we must call our shadowy intellect to life with the pictures of Spiritual Science. That is the abstract way of describing it. The description is concrete when we say: Spirit beings are seeking to come down into Earth existence and must be received. Upheaval upon upheaval will ensue, and Earth existence will at length arrive at social chaos if these beings descended and human existence were to consist only of opposition against them. For these beings wish to be nothing less than the advance guard of what will happen to Earth existence when the Moon reunites once again with the Earth.

Nowadays it may appear comparatively harmless to people when they think only those automatic, lifeless thoughts that arise through comprehension of the mineral world itself and the mineral element's effects in plant, animal, and man. Yes, indeed, people revel in these thoughts; as materialists, they feel good about them; for only such thoughts are conceived today. But imagine that people were to continue thinking in this way, unfolding nothing but such thoughts until the eighth millennium when Moon existence will once more unite with the life of the Earth. What would come about then? The beings I have spoken about will descend gradually to the Earth. Vulcan beings, Vulcan supermen, Venus supermen, Mercury supermen, Sun supermen, and so on will unite themselves with Earth existence. Yet, if human beings persist in their opposition to them, this Earth existence will pass over into chaos in the course of the next few thousand years."

A Picture of Earth-Evolution in the Future, Rudolf Steiner, May 13th, 1921, GA 204

"This quickening to life of the shadow-pictures of the intellect is not only a human but a cosmic event. You will remember the passage in the book *Occult Science* dealing with the time when the human souls ascended to the planets and afterwards descended once more to Earth-existence. I spoke of how the Mars-men, the Jupiter-men and the others descended again to Earth. Now an event of great significance came to pass at the end of the seventies of last century. It is an event that can be described only in the light of facts which are revealed to us in the spiritual world. Whereas in the days of old Atlantis human beings came down to the Earth from Saturn, Jupiter, Mars, and so on—that is to say, beings of soul were drawn into the realm of Earth-existence—since the end of the seventies of last century, other Beings—not of the human order—have been descending to the Earth for the purposes of their further development. From cosmic realms beyond the Earth they come down to the Earth and enter into a definite relationship with human beings. Since the eighties of the nineteenth century, super-Earthly Beings have been seeking to enter the sphere of Earth-existence. Just as the Vulcan-men were the last to come down to the Earth, so now Vulcan Beings are actually coming into the realm of earthly existence. Super-Earthly Beings are already here, and the fact that we are able to have a connected body of Spiritual Science at all today is due to the circumstance that Beings from beyond the Earth are bringing the messages from the spiritual world down into Earth-existence.

But, speaking generally, what is the attitude adopted by the human race? The human race is behaving, if I may put it so very shabbily to these Beings who are appearing from the Cosmos and coming down—slowly and by degrees, it is true—to the Earth. The human race does not concern itself with them; it ignores their existence. And it is this which will plunge the Earth into tragic conditions, for in the course of the next centuries more and more Spiritual Beings will be among us—Beings whose language we ought to understand. And this is possible only if we try to grasp what comes from them: namely, the substance and content of Spiritual Science. They want to give it to us, and they want us to act in the sense of Spiritual Science. Their desire is that Spiritual Science shall be translated into social behavior and action on the Earth.

I repeat, then, that since the last third of the nineteenth century Spiritual Beings from the Cosmos have been coming into our own sphere of existence. Their home is the sphere lying between the Moon and Mercury, but they are already pressing forward into the realm of Earth-existence and seeking to gain a foothold there. And they will be able to find it if human beings are imbued with the thought of their existence. This can also be expressed as I expressed it just now, by saying that our shadowy intellect must be quickened to life by the pictures of Spiritual Science. We are speaking of a concrete fact when we say: Spiritual Beings are seeking to come down into Earth-existence and ought to be willingly received. Catastrophe after catastrophe must ensue, and Earthly life will fall at length into social chaos, if opposition is maintained in human existence to the advent of these Beings. They desire nothing else than to be the advance-guards of what will happen to Earth-existence when the Moon is once again united with the Earth.

Today people may consider it comparatively harmless to elaborate only those automatic, lifeless thoughts which arise in connection with the mineral world and the mineral nature of plant, animal, and man. Materialists revel in such thoughts which are—well—thoughts and nothing more. But try to imagine what will happen if men go on unfolding no other kinds of thoughts until the time is reached in the eighth millennium for the Moon-existence to unite again with the Earth. These Beings of whom I have spoken will gradually come down to the Earth. Vulcan Beings, 'Supermen' of Vulcan, 'Supermen' of Venus, of Mercury, of the Sun, will unite with this Earth-existence. But if human beings persist in nothing but opposition to them, Earth-existence will pass over into chaos in the course of the next few thousand years.

It will be quite possible for the men of Earth, if they so wish, to develop a more and more automatic form of intellect—but that can also happen amid conditions of barbarism. Full and complete manhood, however, cannot come to expression in such a form of intellect, and men will have no relationship to the Beings who would fain come towards them in Earth-existence. And all those Beings of whom men have such an erroneous conception because the shadowy intellect can only grasp the mineral nature, the crudely material nature in the minerals, plants, and animals, nay even in the human kingdom itself—all these thoughts which have no reality will in a trice become substantial realities when the Moon unites again with the Earth. And from the Earth there will spring forth a terrible brood of beings, a brood of automata of an order of existence lying between the mineral and the plant kingdoms and possessed of an overwhelming power of intellect.

This swarm will seize upon the Earth, will spread over the Earth like a network of ghastly, spider-like creatures, of an order lower than that of plant-existence, but possessed of overpowering wisdom. These spidery creatures will be all interlocked with one another, and in their outward movements they will imitate the thoughts that men have spun out of the shadowy intellect that has not allowed itself to be quickened by the new form of Imaginative Knowledge by Spiritual Science. All the thoughts that lack substance and reality will then be endowed with being.

The Earth will be surrounded—as it is now with air and as it sometimes is with swarms of locusts—with a brood of terrible spider-like creatures, half-mineral, half-plant, interweaving with masterly intelligence, it is true, but with intensely evil intent. And in so far as man has not allowed his shadowy intellectual concepts to be quickened to life, his existence will be united not with the Beings who have been trying to descend since the last third of the nineteenth century, but with this ghastly brood of half-mineral, half-plantlike creatures. He will have to live together with these spider-like creatures and to continue his cosmic existence within the order of evolution into which this brood will then enter.

I have been speaking today of a matter upon which we cannot form a lukewarm judgment, for it is part and parcel of the very texture of cosmic existence. The issue at stake is whether human beings will resolve in the present epoch to make themselves worthy to receive what the good Spirits who want to unite with men are bringing down from the Cosmos, or whether men intend to seek their future cosmic existence within the tangled, spider-brood of their own shadowy thoughts."

The Apocalypse of St. John, Rudolf Steiner, June 26, 1908, Lecture III, Nuremberg, GA 104

"Every stage of initiation leads to a higher standpoint of human observation. Even in the first lecture we were able to point out that man progresses step by step, first to what we call the imaginative world, where in the Christian sense he comes to know the "seven seals", then to what we call inspired knowledge, when he hears the "trumpets." and finally to a still higher stage where he is able to understand the true significance and nature of the spiritual beings, the stage of the so-called "vials of wrath." But let us now turn our attention to one particular stage of initiation. Let us imagine that the pupil has reached the stage of initiation where he experiences what was described at the close of our last lecture. We shall imagine him just on the border, between the most ethereal beings of our physical world and the one above it, the astral world, where he is permitted to stand as if on a high peak and look down. What can the pupil see from this first pinnacle of initiation? In spirit he sees all that has happened since the Atlantean flood destroyed ancient Atlantis and the Post-Atlantean man came into existence. He sees how Cultural Periods follow one another up to the time when our Epoch also will come to an end and give place to a new one. Ancient Atlantis came to an end through the waters of the Atlantean flood. Our Epoch will come to an end through what we call the War of All against All, by frightful devastating moral entanglements.

We divide this Fifth Epoch, (7,227 BC-7,894 AD) from the Atlantean Flood to the mighty War of All against All, into seven consecutive Ages of Civilization (2,160 years), as shown in the diagram below. (Diagram 3 and 5)

At one end we imagine the great Atlantean Flood, at the other the great World War (All against all), and we divide this into Seven Cultural Periods [Sub-Ages, Periods of Civilization]. The whole Epoch containing these seven Cultural Periods is again the seventh part of a longer Epoch; so that you have to imagine seven such parts as our Epoch between Flood and War, two after the Great War and four before the Flood. Our Epoch, the Post-Atlantean, is then the Fifth Great Epoch. When the pupil rises to a still higher pinnacle of initiation he surveys these Seven Epochs, each with its seven sub-divisions; he sees them when he arrives at the boundary of the astral and of the spiritual or devachanic world.

We know that when the Atlantean Flood had swept Atlantis away, the ancient Indian civilization came as the First, and that it was succeeded by the ancient Persian civilization [Second]. This was followed by the Assyrian-Babylonian-Chaldaic-Egyptian-Hebrew civilization [Third], this by the Fourth Age of Civilization, the Graeco-Latin, which was followed by the Fifth, the one in which we are now living. The Sixth, which will follow ours, will be in a certain sense the fruit of what we have to develop in the way of spiritual civilization. The Seventh Age of Civilization will run its course before the War of All against All. Here we see this terrible devastation of civilization approaching, we see also the small group of people who have succeeded in taking the spiritual principle into themselves and are rescued from the general destruction which comes through egoism.

And if we follow this path, we shall bring into the Sixth Post-Atlantean Period the true spiritual life of wisdom and of love. The spiritual wisdom we have acquired will become the impulse of love in the Sixth Post-Atlantean Period, which is represented by the community expressing itself even in its name, the community of brotherly love, or Philadelphia. All these names are carefully chosen. Man will develop his "I" to the necessary height, so that he will become independent and in freedom show love towards all other beings in the Sixth Post-Atlantean Period, which is represented by the community at Philadelphia. In this way the spiritual life of the Sixth Post-Atlantean Period will be prepared. We shall then have found the individual "I" within us in a higher degree, so that no external power can any longer play upon us if we do not wish it; so that we can close and no one without our will can open, and if we open no opposing power can close. These are the Keys of David. For this reason, he who inspires the letter says that he has the Keys of David:

> "And to the Angel of the community in Philadelphia write: These things saith he that is holy, he that is true, he that hath the key of David, he that openeth, and no man shutteth; and shutteth and no man openeth. ... Behold, I have set before thee an open door, and no man can shut it." (*Revelation* 3:7)

In the Seventh Post-Atlantean Period those who have found this spiritual life will flock around the great Leader; it will unite them around this great Leader. They will already belong so far to the spiritual life that they will be distinguished from those who have fallen away, who are lukewarm, "neither cold nor hot." The little flock which has found spirituality will understand him who may then say, when he makes himself known, "I am he who contains in himself the true final Being towards which everything is steering." For this final Being is described by the word, "Amen."

> "And unto the Angel of the church of Laodicea write: Thus saith the Amen, he who in his being presents the nature of the end." (*Revelation* 3:14)

Reading the Pictures of the Apocalypse, Rudolf Steiner, Lecture I, 1907, GA 104a

"We remember that our present fifth root race was preceded by the Atlantean race, which was destroyed by a flood. What will destroy the fifth race? The fifth race has a special task: the development of egotism. This egotism will, at the same time, create what causes the downfall of the fifth root race. A small part of humankind will live toward the sixth main race; a larger part will not yet have found the light within. Because egotism is the fundamental power in the soul, the War of All against All will rage within this larger part of humanity. As the Lemurian race found its end through the power of fire, the Atlantean through water, so will the fifth race find its destruction in conflict between selfish, egoistic powers in the War of All against All. This line of evolution will descend deeper and deeper; when it arrives at the bottom everyone will rage against everyone else. A small part of humankind will escape this, just as a small part escaped during the destruction of the Atlantean race. It is up to every individual to find a connection to spiritual life in order to be one of those to go over into the sixth root race. Mighty revolutions stand before humankind; they are described in the *Apocalypse*.

I will cite only a very special passage. The sixth letter must be addressed to a community where Budhi [Life-Spirit] is especially cultivated. What does that mean? If Manas [Spirit-Self] is especially cultivated, and if the human being has become a knower, then what we previously knew will pass over into our living feelings; it becomes for us a natural, given, feeling. It becomes a passion for us. If you realize that justice should prevail, that justice should live, if you realize that humankind cannot live without the beautiful and the good, then you are on the way to developing Budhi. If higher things have become your second nature, if your soul is fully permeated with enthusiasm for the beautiful and the true, then you are on the path to Budhi. Budhi takes its substance from the realm of feelings; and Atman [Spirit-Man, Spirit-Human] from the realm of the will. And when humankind finally reaches the point where it has made enthusiasm for the good into a reality, then what is called the Christian ideal of brotherhood will have appeared. This sixth territory can receive its name only from the ideal of brotherhood, and "Philadelphia" is the city of brotherly love. If you read the relevant passage, you will see the city described this way: "I know your works. Behold, I set before you an open door, which no one is able to shut; I know that you have but little power, and yet you have kept my word and have not denied my name." (*Revelation* 3:8) They did not deny the name that comes from fraternal duty.

The seventh letter is taken from the realm of Atman, the Atman or breath of the human being. When we have come as far as the physical breath we take in, when the I has worked down into the physical body—perhaps you know that in Christian esotericism this is designated by the word "amen"—then the esotericist, when speaking of this, will refer to the "amen," and to the Angel of the Church (community) in Laodicea write: "The words of the amen, the faithful and true witness, the beginning of God's creation." (*Revelation* 3:14)

When the fifth seal is opened, we are told something very significant: "When he opened the fifth seal, I saw under the altar the souls of those who had been slain for the word of God and for the witness they had borne ..." (*Revelation* 6:9) What happens to a soul that develops itself up to the fifth step? It is strangled in its lower soul; the impurities that cling to it are done away with, and the soul thereby appears clothed in innocence: "And they were each given a white robe ..." (*Revelation* 6:11) The soul is white; it has become innocent when it has developed to the fifth step. (Diagram 5)

The Fifth Epoch is called to find again the spiritual world behind sense existence; and Theosophy must reach the point where it can lead people increasingly to permeate all knowledge with the principle of Christ. The Fifth Epoch can feel, to begin with, only as a perspective, that this new science is approaching, that humanity will understand in a new way what Zarathustra meant when he spoke of Ahura Mazdao.

The ancient wisdom of Zarathustra will appear again in a new form in the Sixth Age [7th Post-Atlantean Period]. Finally, the age [7th Post-Atlantean

Period] of the holy Rishis will come again in a new form. There may be only a small band of people who understand Theosophy in our age; there may be only the smallest of groups present to hear the re-enlivened wisdom of Zarathustra in the Sixth Age [Post-Atlantean Period]; and, finally there may be only a fraction remaining for the Seventh Age [Post-Atlantean Period]. The further course of human evolution will be such that more and more people will gather together who will understand what Zarathustra proclaimed.

Then an Age will come upon the Earth when the victors will be those who lead the War of All against All. But the souls who will have been preserved from the Sixth Age [Post-Atlantean Period] must found a new culture after the War of All against All. The Seventh Age [Post-Atlantean Period] will have neither people who glow with enthusiasm for the spiritual, nor those who glow with enthusiasm for sense existence; even for that these people will be too blasé. Very little of the Indian, the first culture [Post-Atlantean Period], will be perceptible on the Earth in the Seventh Age [Post-Atlantean Period]. But these souls from the Sixth Age [Post-Atlantean Period] when earned up into the spiritual world, purified and Christened, will walk as it were etherically, no longer touching the Earth, while humanity then will be able to master what the entire culture of Earth has to offer. The Seventh Age [Post-Atlantean Period] will be such that here below on the Earth, people living in increasingly dense and hardened bodies will make the greatest discoveries and inventions. In the Seventh Age [Post-Atlantean Period], human beings wholly entangled in matter will no longer have to fear much from Theosophy, for on Earth there will no longer be much to find of those transformed human beings who will have increasingly spiritualized themselves in the Sixth Age [Post-Atlantean Period] by absorbing Theosophy. The people who have understood the call of the master today will be carried over into a distant future. The key will be turned into the Sixth Cultural Age [Post-Atlantean Period]. Those who have heard the call will be the founders of a new humanity. If only a few people are entangled with matter, the community of Laodicea will not last long. It lies within the free will of every human being to belong to either the community of Philadelphia or the community of Laodicea.

Theosophists make themselves into living recipients of what Moses and Paul were given in the revelation of Yahweh-Christ. Therefore, we read in the fifth letter in the *Apocalypse* how the people of the Fifth Cultural Epoch [Post-Atlantean Period] are those who truly take into themselves what will later be self-evident for the cultural age of the community of Philadelphia [Sixth Post-Atlantean Period]. The wisdom of the Fifth Cultural Age [Post-Atlantean Period] will blossom forth as a flower of love in the Sixth Cultural Age [Post-Atlantean Period].

With the community at Philadelphia, the Sixth Age [Post-Atlantean Period] will begin. Except for these spiritual human beings, the rest of humankind will be entirely wrapped up in social life, submerged in materialism that will be constantly growing stronger. People will master the forces of nature to a high degree, as we have seen with wireless telegraphy and aeronautics. It is not without consequences whether the air is filled with spiritual thoughts or with thoughts of material needs. This will engulf our entire planet. We are looking into an age when humanity will intrude in large measure into air and light-filled space. What will be the fruits of this age? Seen in their true form it can be said that these electromagnetic waves will work back into the forces of the Earth during a certain age. Then, according to good and evil, Earthquakes and Earth tremors will appear as the effects of human deeds. "When he opened the sixth seal I looked, and behold, there was a great earthquake; and the Sun became black as sackcloth." (*Revelation* 6:12) When the feelings of human beings are carried into the air, they change all of nature and something like a meteor shower appears. In this way human beings unleash the forces of nature, but their achievements do not go unpunished. When we see this, it appears at the same time that humanity finds its own destruction within these unleashed forces of nature. But those who unite themselves with the spirit appear as the "sealed" human beings. Such people must take into themselves the teachings that concern the spirit and can reach humanity. What human beings take into themselves as spiritual substance and teaching will be their soul and spiritual life blood in the future. It will be the light that will ray forth from them as spirit."

Reading the Pictures of the Apocalypse, Rudolf Steiner, Lecture IV, 1907, GA 104a

"In the last lecture we showed how the *Revelation of Saint John* prophetically points to the cycle of human evolution lying between the great upheaval upon our Earth which the legends of various peoples describe as a flood; and geology, the glacial period on the one hand, and that event which we designate as the War of All against All on the other. In the Epoch [15,120-year Epoch] between these two events lies everything prophetically referred to in the *Apocalypse*—that book which reveals to us the beings of past ages in order to show what is to fire our will and our impulses for the future. We have also seen how we ourselves, in the spiritual movement to which we belong, should consider the words of the so-called fifth letter as a summons to action, to work. We have seen that we ought to follow that Being with the seven Spirits of God and the seven stars. Then we saw how, through this spiritual movement, the next Age is prepared which is represented by the community of Philadelphia [Sixth Post-Atlantean Period], the Age when—among all those who have understood the word of the summons—there is to be that brotherly love over the whole Earth which is described in the *Gospel of John*. Afterwards another Age, the Seventh [Post-Atlantean Period] will follow, which the writer of the *Apocalypse* describes by saying that on the one hand there is placed all that is bad in the community representing the Seventh Age, that is lukewarm, neither hot nor cold, that could not warm to the spiritual life and hence must fall away, and on the other hand those who have understood the word of invitation, those who will form his following who says, "I am the Amen," that is: I am he who unites in himself the goal of the human being, who contains the Christ principle in himself.

Now let us keep for a later occasion all that could be added in further explanation of the several letters and in justification of the several names of the cities. Today we shall pass on in our studies to that which presents itself to the pupil when he advances to the next stage of initiation. We were confronted by the seven sub-ages of the present cycle of humanity, and we have said that this entire cycle with its seven Sub-Ages [Post-Atlantean Period] is itself a small cycle contained in a longer period also containing Seven Epochs. Our Epoch, which embraces Seven Ages, was preceded by the Atlantean Epoch, during which were prepared the races whose echoes still exist. When the Seventh Age of our present Epoch is at an end, it will be followed by another Epoch again consisting of seven parts. The present Epoch is preparing indirectly for the following one, so that we may say, our Age of Civilization will gradually pass over into one of brotherly love [Sixth Post-

Atlantean Period], when a comparatively small part of humanity will have understood the spiritual life and will have prepared the spirit and attitude of brotherly love. That civilization will then again divide off a smaller portion of human beings who will survive the event which will have such a destructive effect upon our epoch, namely, the War of All against All. In this universal destructive element, there will be everywhere individuals who lift themselves above the rest of warring humanity, individuals who have understood the spiritual life and who will form the foundation for a new and different world in the Sixth Epoch.

Those who hear the voice which calls them to progress will survive the great period of destruction—the War of All against All—and appear in new bodies which will be quite different from those of the present day.

In the course of thousands of years, the external physiognomy changes and after the great War of All against All, mankind will have quite a different form. Today he is so formed that in a certain sense he can conceal the good and evil in his nature. The human physiognomy already betrays a good deal, it is true, and one who understands this will be able to read much from the features.

Upon the forehead and in the whole physiognomy it will be written whether the person is good or evil. He will show in his face what is contained in his inmost soul. What a man has developed within himself, whether he has exercised good or evil impulses, will be written on his forehead. After the great War of All against All there will be two kinds of human beings. Those who had previously tried to follow the call to the spiritual life, who cultivated the spiritualizing and ennobling of their inner spiritual life, will show this inward life on their faces and express it in their gestures and the movements of their hands. And those who have turned away from the spiritual life, represented by the community of Laodicea, who were lukewarm, neither warm nor cold, will pass into the following Epoch as those who retard human evolution, who preserve the backward forces of evolution which have been left behind. They will show the evil passions, impulses, and instincts hostile to the spiritual in an ugly, unintelligent, evil-looking countenance. In their gestures and hand-movements, in everything they do, they will present an outer image of the ugliness in their soul. Just as humanity has separated into races and communities, in the future it will divide into two great streams, the good and the evil. And what is in their souls will be outwardly manifest, they will no longer be able to hide it."

Reading the Pictures of the Apocalypse, Rudolf Steiner, Lecture VIII, 1907, GA 104a

"We have said repeatedly that our Epoch will end, when the Seventh Age [Post-Atlantean Period] has passed away, by the War of All against All, but this war must really be pictured quite differently from the way we have been accustomed to think of war. We must bear in mind the foundation, the real cause of this war. This foundation or cause is the increase of egoism, of self-seeking and selfishness on the part of man. Thus the "I" will be the pledge for the highest goal of man. But at the same time, if it does not discover love, if it hardens within itself, it is the tempter that plunges him into the Abyss. For it is that which separates men from one another which brings them to the great War of All against All, not only to the war of nation against nation (for the conception of a nation will then no longer have the significance it possesses today) but to the war of each single person against every other person in every branch of life; to the war of class against class, of caste against caste and sex against sex. Thus, in every field of life the "I" will become the apple of discord; and hence we may say that it can lead on the one hand to the highest and on the other hand to the lowest.

The so-called Seventh Age [Post-Atlantean Period] will be of very little importance. We are now living in the Fifth Age of Civilization [Post-Atlantean Period]; then follows the Sixth, from which will proceed a number of people full of understanding for the spiritual world, filled with the spirit of brotherly love, which results from spiritual knowledge. The ripest fruit of our present civilization will appear in the Sixth Age [Post-Atlantean Period]. And that which follows it will be what is lukewarm, neither warm nor cold; the Seventh Age [Post-Atlantean Period] is something like an overripe fruit, which outlasts the War of All against All, but contains no principle of progress.

Just as it happened at that time with the fifth race, that it provided men who were capable of development and with the sixth and seventh, that they experienced a descent, so will it also be in our Epoch. We are now looking with great longing towards the Sixth Civilization [Post-Atlantean Period], to that which must be described as developing out of the spiritual marriage between West and East. The sixth stage will be the foundation for the new civilizations which will arise after the great War of All against All; just as our civilization arose after the Atlantean Epoch. On the other hand, the seventh race of culture will be characterized by the lukewarm. This Seventh Age [Post-Atlantean Period] will continue into the new Epoch, just as the sixth and seventh races of the Atlantean Epoch continued into our Epoch as races hardened and stiffened. After the War of All against All, there will be two streams in humanity: on the one hand the stream of Philadelphia will survive with the principle of progress, of inner freedom, of brotherly love, a small group drawn from every tribe and nation; and on the other hand, the great mass of all those who are lukewarm, the remains of those who are now becoming lukewarm (Laodicea).

After the great War of All against All, gradually the evil stream will be led over to good by the good race, by the good stream. This will be one of the principal tasks after the great War of All against All; to rescue what can be rescued from those who after the great war will only have the impulse to fight one another and to allow the "I" to express itself in the most external egoism.

For after the great War of All against All, the good will have to make every possible effort to rescue the evil during the period in which this will still be possible. This will not merely be a work of education, such as exists today, but occult forces will co-operate. For in this next great Epoch men will understand how to set occult forces in motion. The good will have the task of working upon their brothers of the evil movement.

The most capable must be chosen and prepared to live beyond the period of the great War of All against All when men will confront those who bear in their countenances the sign of evil; they must be so prepared that as much good force as possible will flow into humanity. It will still be possible for those bodies, which are to a certain extent soft, to be transformed after the War of All against All by the converted souls, by the souls who will still be led to the good in this last Epoch. In this way much will be accomplished. The "Good" would not be so great a good if it were not to grow through the conquest of evil. Love would not be so intense if it had not to become love so great as to be able even to overcome the wickedness in the countenances of evil men.

Thus, you see how present-day humanity will pass into the new Epoch beyond the War of All against All, just as that root-race of the Atlanteans lived over into our Epoch and founded our civilizations. After the great War of All against All humanity will develop in seven consecutive stages. We have already seen how that which is said concerning the opening of the seven seals in the *Apocalypse of John* gives us the character of the seven consecutive civilizations after the great war. Then when this civilization—which can only be seen by the initiates in the astral world and in its symbolism—has run its course, a new epoch will begin for our Earth development in which again new forms will appear. And this new Epoch, which will follow the one just described, is symbolized in the *Apocalypse of John* by the sounding of the seven trumpets. Just as the Epoch after the great War of All against All is characterized by the seven seals, because the seer can only see it today from the astral world, so by the sounding of the trumpets is characterized the stage of civilization which follows, because man can only perceive it from the true spiritual world [Devachan] where the tones of the spheres sound forth. In the astral world man perceives the world in pictures, in symbols, in Devachan he perceives it in inspiring music; and in this Devachan is contained the climax, as it were, of what is revealed concerning what follows the great War of All against All.

Ages of Civilization

I	II	III	IV	V	VI	VIII

1 2 3 4 5 6 7
a-------b

Thus, if we represent it in a diagram we have our seven Ages of Civilization [First-Seventh Post-Atlantean Periods, Sub-Epochs] in the space between the letters a-b, so that we have the ancient Indian civilization as the First, the ancient Persian as the Second, the Assyrian-Babylonian-Chaldean-Egyptian-Jewish [as the Third], the Graeco-Latin [as the Fourth], and our own as the Fifth stage [ours] of the Post-Atlantean Epoch. The figure IV would be the Atlantean Epoch, (a) the great flood [7,227 BC] by which this comes to an end, and (b) the great War of All against All [7,894 AD]. Then follows a 15,120 year Epoch of seven stages (VI) which is represented by the seven seals, then follows another 15,120 year Epoch (VII) also containing seven stages, represented by the seven trumpets. Here again lies the boundary of our physical Earth development. This is seen in relationship to the current Platonic Great Year; or Precession of the Equinox; a cycle of 25,920 years, that is determined by the equal 30° sectors of the constellations that are seen on the Eastern horizon at sunrise as it passes backwards through the twelve signs of the Zodiac in a complete cycle. Although, the time periods of the 6th and 7th Epochs is approximate as the relationship to time, as we know it, could undergo a change due to terrestrial events following the return of the Moon to the Earth in the 8th millennium AD. Therefore, it should be considered in its relationship to the surrounding 12-fold Zodiac. Then follows an Epoch of seven stages (VI) which is represented by the seven seals, then follows another (VII) also containing seven stages, represented by the seven trumpets. Here again lies the boundary of our physical Earth development.

For if we have had to say that already in the Sixth Post-Atlantean Period men will show good and evil on their faces, we shall have to say all the more of the Seventh Post-Atlantean Period that the form of man and the forms of all the other beings will be an expression of good and evil to a much higher degree than in the Sixth Post-Atlantean Period. All matter will bear the stamp of the spirit. There will be absolutely nothing in this Seventh Post-Atlantean Period that can be hidden in any way. Even those belonging to the Sixth Post-Atlantean Period will be unable to hide anything from him who has the necessary vision. An evil man will express his evil, a good man will express the good that is within him; but in the Seventh Post-Atlantean Period it will be quite impossible by speech to hide what is in the soul. Thought will no longer remain dumb so that it can be hidden, for when the soul thinks, its thought will ring forth outwardly. It will then be just as thought is already to the Initiates today. To them thought now rings out in Devachan. But this Devachan will have descended into the physical world, just as the astral world will have descended into the physical world in the Sixth Post-Atlantean Period. Even now the Sixth Epoch can be found in the astral world and the Seventh Epoch in the heavenly world. The Sixth Epoch is the descended astral world, that is to say, the images, the expressions, the manifestations of it.

The Seventh Epoch will be the descended heavenly world, the expression of it. And then the Earth will have reached the goal of its physical evolution. The Earth, together with all its beings, will then change into an astral heavenly body. Physical substance, as such, will disappear. The part which until then had been able to spiritualize itself, will pass over into the spirit, into astral substance. Imagine all the beings of the Earth who up to that time have been able to express what is good, noble, intellectual and beautiful in their external material form; who will bear an expression of Christ Jesus in their countenances, whose words will manifest Christ Jesus, for they will ring out as resounding thoughts—all these will have the power to dissolve what they have within them as physical matter, as warm water dissolves salt. Everything physical will pass over into an astral globe. But those who up to that time have not progressed so far as to be a material and corporeal expression of what is noble, beautiful, intellectual, and good, will not have the power to dissolve matter; for them matter will remain. They will become hardened in matter; they will retain material form. At this point in the Earth's evolution there will be an ascent into the spirit of forms which will live in the astral and which will separate from themselves another material globe, a globe which will contain beings unfit for the ascent because they are unable to dissolve the material part. In this way our Earth will advance towards its future. Through the souls gradually refining matter from within, the substance of the Earth will become more and more refined until it receives the power to dissolve. Then will come the time when the insoluble part will be ejected as a special planet. In the course of Seven Ages, that which has hardened itself in matter will be driven out, and the power which drives it out will be the opposite force to that which will have forced the good beings upward.

What, then, will they have used to dissolve matter? The power of love gained through the Christ-Principle. Beings become capable of dissolving matter through taking love into their souls. The more the soul is warmed by love, the more powerfully will it be able to work on matter; it will spiritualize the whole Earth and transform it into an astral globe. But just as love dissolves matter, as warm water dissolves salt, so will the opposite of love press down— again throughout seven stages everything which has not become capable of fulfilling the Earth mission."

Lectures to Priests: The Apocalypse, Rudolf Steiner, Lecture V, September 5, 1924, Dornach, GA 346

"This is something which will arise evermore during the Fifth Post-Atlantean Period, namely, people will see death walking alongside them. To put it even more concretely: men will perceive an intimate fire process in themselves which is connected with the development of the Consciousness Soul. They will experience this development of waking consciousness like a kind of fire process which consumes them, especially at the moments when they pass over from sleeping to waking consciousness. The Consciousness Soul is a very spiritual thing, and spiritual things always consume material ones. The Consciousness Soul consumes material and etheric things in human beings through a kind of intimate fire process or transformation process.

This is something which men will perceive more and more in the course of this Fifth Post-Atlantean Period. People will see all of this in a certain way during the Sixth Post-Atlantean Period. The Sun and the stars and planets in their present form will have fallen down from the heavens. One will see the working and weaving of spirit where the materially abstract stars shine today. Thus, the way that men see themselves will change a great deal in the course of the Fifth Post-Atlantean Period and the way they see the whole world around them will change greatly in the course of the Sixth.

If we look back at the last big event which separates the Atlantean Epoch from the present Age, which is now in its Fifth Cultural Period, we have what is known as the ice age or flood between the two, the sinking of Atlantis and the rising of new continents.

We are living in the Fifth Post-Atlantean Period, a Sixth one will follow and a Seventh one will follow. The catastrophe which then separates us from the next large Epoch which will come [after] the Fifth Epoch [transitions into] from the Sixth Epoch will not just be an external event in nature like the Ice Age or Flood was. This separation of the Fifth [Epoch] from the Sixth Epoch will become manifest in a more moral way. As I have often mentioned, a War of All against All or a moral catastrophe will separate the Fifth Epoch from the large Sixth Earth Epoch."

Lectures to Priests: The Apocalypse, Rudolf Steiner, Lecture VIII, GA 346

"And so we see, if the apocalypticer saw all of that, and he did see it, for he saw that the true unfolding of Christianity is a Sun event, and he saw the development of this abominable possession by Sun demons. That hovered before him. And the entry of Michael into the spiritual evolution of humanity at the end of the 19th century and the appearance of the etheric Christ in the first half of the 20th century, will be followed by the appearance of the Sun Demon before the end of this century.

After the second 666 stood in the sign of that great upheaval in Europe, which was begun by the crusades and which had its outer fact in the appearance and destruction of the Templar knights, everything from the Sun genius [Michael] which is trying to create true Christianity works on, as does everything from Sorat which is trying to work against it. And we have the age of the third 666 as the year 1998. We are coming to the end of this century, when Sorat will again lift his head from the waters of evolution very strongly, where he will be the adversary of that vision of the Christ which prepared human beings will already have in the first half of the 20th century through the appearance of the etheric Christ. It will then take almost two thirds of a century until Sorat raises his head in a mighty way.

When the first 666 went by, Sorat was still hidden in the evolutionary course of events; one didn't see him in an external form; he lived in the deeds of Arabism, although initiates could see him. When the second 666 came he already showed himself in the thinking and feeling of the tortured Templars. He will show himself before the end of this century already, and he will appear in a great many people as a being by whom they will be possessed. One will see people coming up to one and one will not be able to believe that they are really human beings. They will develop in a very strange way even outwardly. They will be intensive, strong natures outwardly with fierce features and a destructive rage in their emotions; they will have a face in which one will see a kind of a beast's face outwardly. Sorat men will also be recognizable outwardly; they will be those who not only ridicule spiritual things, they will fight it in the most terrible way and they will want to thrust it down into a cesspool. One will see that what is concentrated in a small region in present-day Russian Communism will be inserted into the whole Earth evolution of humanity. The path is being prepared for the entry of demons who are the followers of the great Sorat demon."

Becoming Angels on Future Jupiter

Rudolf Steiner's cosmology explains that the Earth, as we know it, has gone through three prior "planetary incarnations" in the past and that Earth will go through three more in the future. These past planetary incarnations, Old Saturn, Old Sun, Old Moon are distinct in their own time and space, but they also interpenetrate the Earth in our current time by leaving behind their "donations/sacrifices" that have eventually become our mineral, plant, and animal kingdoms on Earth. Various beings from the nine hierarchies (Seraphim, Cherubim, Thrones, Kyriotetes, Dynamis, Elohim, Archai, Archangels, Angels) have donated substances that other lower ranking hierarchies used to experience a type of "human" condition in the ancient past. This simultaneously shared substance also goes through further changes during the three planetary incarnations of Old Saturn, Old Sun, and Old Moon before becoming the substance of the mineral, plant, and animal kingdoms on Earth. These donations, or sacrifices, of the divine hierarchies become the substances that support our human life on Earth.

This process is called heterochrony and represents what might be imagined as the creation of the Earth's three physical dimensions of length, width, and depth or the kingdoms of mineral, plant, and animal. These kingdoms of nature (dimensions) of past hierarchical activity also contributed to the creation of human consciousness; specifically, the three soul aspects of humans on Earth—willing, feeling, and thinking. When the human ego (I Am) can gain control of these three soul aspects, it also becomes possible to pull down advanced human capacities from the three future incarnations of the Earth called Future Jupiter, Future Venus, and Future Vulcan. These future states of consciousness will be developed by humans when they evolve into the three spiritual aspects of human evolution—Spirit-Self (Manas), Life-Spirit (Buddhi), and Spirit Human (Atman). These future incarnations of the Earth are also named in Vedic literature as Nirvana, Paranirvana, and Mahaparanirvana which are called in Christianity the three levels of heaven. Or as Saint Paul says in *2 Corinthians* 12:2-4:

"I know a man in Christ who fourteen years ago was caught up to the third heaven. Whether it was in the body or out of the body I do not know—God knows—was caught up to paradise and heard inexpressible things, things that no one is permitted to tell."

Or in *2 Enoch,* we hear of Enoch being caught up into the third heaven:

"And they took me from there, and they brought me up to the third heaven, and set me down there. Then I looked downward, and I saw Paradise. And that place is inconceivably pleasant."

The three heavens being referred to are called in Esoteric Christianity: Future Jupiter, Future Venus, and Future Vulcan. There is no "time" or "space" in the spiritual world, so these future realms are somewhat like the ancient incarnations of the Earth that exist concurrently on our Earth. The three heavens also manifest in the present through futuristic heterochrony. Time past and time future are already conquered by Christ ("I am the Alpha and the Omega, the First and Last, the Beginning and the End." *Revelation* 22:13) and the Holy Trinity through the manifestation of the divine plan for the spiritual evolution of humanity. Or, as Rudolf Steiner said in *Cosmic and Human Metamorphoses*, GA 175:

"So that today, instead of using the more complicated expression and saying: 'We are in connection with the Hierarchy of the Angels'; we can simply say: 'We are in connection with that which is to come to us in the future—our Spirit-Self.' And instead of saying that we are in connection with the Archangels, we can say: 'We are in connection with what is to come to us in the future, as our Life-Spirit,' and so on."

Only Dr. Steiner's descriptions and characterizations of the seven planetary incarnations of the Earth create a comprehensive and applicable system that explains the entire evolution of humanity from beginning to end with the accompanying correspondences to physical, etheric, astral, and spiritual components of the world and humanity. Steiner's explanations concerning the Divine Hierarchies are enough to establish a new religion that relinks to our spiritual home from whence we came, and to which we shall return. Much of what the ancients understood through their natural clairvoyance about the spiritual world is contained in Spiritual Science-- Steiner's Anthroposophy. This natural wisdom transcends theology, mythology, materialistic science, and intellectual speculation. Steiner's own cosmology is a new "Theory of Everything" that is more coherent and comprehensive than any other that currently exists. His spiritual scientific discoveries and predictions are perhaps the most important in our time and have repeatedly been proven to be true. These spiritual scientific realities need to be further researched and brought forward to establish Steiner's position as one of the great thinkers in astrophysics, astronomy, psychology, art, drama, history, theology, and philosophy—a genius polymath, a true Renaissance Man. His Spiritual Science is more valid and provable than materialistic scientific theories that fade away quickly as they are supplanted by new godless theories that are inadequate and remove the human being from the equation without giving any consideration to the unseen world of the divine. Science has become "machine intelligence" that is devoid of God, human consideration, Angelic influence, or anything beyond materialistic nihilism and entropy.

Spiritual Science shows us that Future Jupiter is the Christian Heaven, the Buddhist Tushita Heaven, the Vedic Nirvana, Enlightenment, Transcendence, the Anthroposophic Spirit-Self, the Theosophic realm of Manas, the world of Moral Imagination, the home of Angels, and what St. John called the New Jerusalem or Heavenly Jerusalem. Just as the *Bible* tells us, we build this new world (heaven) with every thought, word, and deed that we create on Earth. If the action is moral and born from love, the spiritual aspirant creates a new "living stone" that builds a spiritual edifice (mansion) in heaven, the Future Jupiter. Christ is the "living stone" that is the foundation of this temple of New Jerusalem that has the Tree of Life growing in the center giving forth the "rivers of life" that flow out in four directions. This is clearly indicated in the following quote from *1 Peter* 2:5:

> "You also, like living stones, are being built into a spiritual house to be a holy priesthood, offering spiritual sacrifices acceptable to God through Jesus Christ."

Rudolf Steiner says essentially the same thing in spiritual scientific terms in GA 10:

> "On Future Jupiter [heaven], your spiritual home has been formed by yourself with full consciousness. This formation of a spiritual home is known in the speech of Spiritual Science as 'the building of the [spiritual] hut.'"

This spiritual "hut" can also be a temple, palace, mansion, house, hall of wisdom, or spiritual edifice of any type. Jesus Christ tells us this in his own words:

"In my Father's house are many mansions: if it were not so, I would have told you. I go to prepare a place for you. And if I go and prepare a place for you, I will come again, and receive you unto myself; that where I am, there ye may be also. And whither I go ye know, and the way ye know." (*John* 14: 1-7)

Rudolf Steiner's indications and teachings do not conflict with the *Bible* but, in fact, enhance one's understanding of the mystery wisdom that is often hidden in the words. Steiner's view of heaven agrees with the *Bible* in principle and detail; plus, Spiritual Science gives us much more information about the manifestation and reality of "things unseen." Christ's teachings are often misunderstood or taken as an analogy instead of spiritual reality. Steiner elucidates those ideas and makes them as real as provable science and shows the way they fit into the Divine Plan of the Maha-Manvantara, the great cycle of seven incarnations of the Earth. Once the aspirant understands what Dr. Steiner has said about Future Jupiter, one can clearly see that it is an expansion of what Christ told us in the *Bible*:

"Consequently, you are no longer foreigners and strangers, but fellow citizens with God's people and also members of his household, built on the foundation of the apostles and prophets, with Christ Jesus himself as the chief cornerstone. In him the whole building is joined together and rises to become a holy temple in the Lord. And in him you too are being built together to become a dwelling in which God lives by his Spirit." (*Ephesians* 2: 21-22)

In *1 Corinthians* 3:9, we hear Paul describe the building of the new temple of man in the future in much the same way that Steiner describes it in his teachings:

"For we are laborers together with God: ye are God's husbandry, ye are God's building. According to the grace of God which is given unto me, as a wise master-builder, I have laid the foundation, and another buildeth thereon. But let every man take heed how he buildeth thereupon. For other foundation can no man lay than that is laid, which is Jesus Christ. Now if any man build upon this foundation gold, silver, precious stones, wood, hay, stubble; every man's work shall be made manifest: for the day shall declare it, because it shall be revealed by fire; and the fire shall try every man's work of what sort it is. If any man's work abide which he hath built thereupon, he shall receive a reward. Know ye not that ye are the temple of God, and that the Spirit of God dwelleth in you? If any man defile the temple of God, him shall God destroy; for the temple of God is holy, which temple ye are."

Through Spiritual Science we also know exactly what our actions on Earth will create on Future Jupiter. Every moral action accomplished on Earth will help build a spiritual temple with Christ in heaven; but they will also create the mineral, plant, animal, and human kingdoms found on Future Jupiter. Humans are co-creative partners with the spiritual hierarchies in creating Future Jupiter [heaven]. We are, at this moment, spiritual beings creating the future world we will live in. This was understood by Christians because the human body was considered sacred, holy ground from which spiritual substance is created to make Heavenly Jerusalem: "Know ye not that ye are the Temple of God, and that the Spirit of God dwelleth in you?" (*Corinthians* 3:16)

We are currently creating the "living stones" of spiritual morality and love that are constructing our new "mansions" in heaven, as well as the kingdoms of nature of the Future Jupiter incarnation of the Earth. As Christ said in *John* 18:36—"My kingdom is not of this world..." Christ only came to Earth once in a physical body to teach humans the "way, the truth, and the life" as a perfect example for humans to follow so that the Heavenly Jerusalem could be created from human moral action through love that is given freely. Christ was building His Father's heaven through His deeds. He was building Future Jupiter and laid the foundation stone upon which we can add living stones (fiery stones) to create the Temple of Wisdom and Love in the spiritual world—the Future Jupiter. If we fail to create these moral living stones, we simply add to the Eighth Sphere of evil dross by making immoral garbage for Future Jupiter's Moon. The unacceptable, immoral deeds created on Earth comprise the "hell-realm" of the Eighth Sphere that will metamorphose into a Moon filled with rejected slag and animal-humans revolving around Future Jupiter—Heavenly Jerusalem. Everything we do now creates the Future Jupiter (heaven) for good or ill. As the *Bible* tells us:

"Do not lay up for yourselves treasures on Earth...but lay up for yourselves treasures in heaven... for where your treasure is, there your heart will be also." (*Matthew* 6:19-21)

Many students of Spiritual Science won't talk about, or think about, the Future Jupiter incarnation of Earth because they believe it is scary and overwhelming.

They forget that time doesn't exist in the spiritual world, neither does space as we know it. Therefore, what we do now is essentially the author of our future home, environment, body, and spiritual consciousness. We don't just live life to be judged and sent to some place like heaven, hell, purgatory, or some other realm by some hidden being who controls karma. We create our own karma and should be able to know in advance what we are building for the future from the karma we are creating now. Christ as the Lord of Karma should be as close as our own conscience, speaking to us constantly and guiding our actions towards a brighter future in heaven. Many are building a future world that is terrible and frightening with their immoral deeds of selfishness and vice. Steiner describes the future condition of both the moral humans who become Angels and the immoral animal-humans who fail to advance to Angelic consciousness on Future Jupiter. It is up to each individual to determine which direction they will go with their own spiritual evolution. Once we realize the importance of every single deed on Earth, we then will begin to acknowledge the power we have to make a new world in the image of heaven or hell.

Throughout Dr. Steiner's over six-thousand lectures and numerous books we hear much about the Future Jupiter and the way it is connected to our current Earth incarnation. The selections from Rudolf Steiner's books that are found below may seem extensive and too long to read for most people, but Steiner has given us so much information about this future heaven that it had to be included in this presentation to create a complete picture of the future. Even descriptions of what the human body will metamorphose into are given in these selections.

Have you ever wondered what an Angel looks like? Steiner gives us a detailed description of the Angel that you will become during the Future Jupiter incarnation, if you have learned to turn wisdom into love through freedom during the current Earth incarnation. We may become the Angels of Future Jupiter and perhaps eventually evolve into Archangels on Future Venus, and Archai on Future Vulcan. Much of what is described by Steiner goes beyond any view that theologists and spiritual teachers have provided for us. Steiner even tells us about new spiritual thought that will come into existence in the future that is beyond the current purview of Anthroposophy. Some of these indications will now be presented in a chart format so that the spiritual correspondences are made clear.

On Earth	Will Become on Jupiter
Thoughts-words-speech	Mineral formations-rocks-solid forms
Human feelings	Inner warmth-oceans-fluids
Human willpower	Beings of Future Jupiter
Words of external science	Atoms of Jupiter

Words of Spiritual Science	Vegetation life-plant kingdom
Dreamer of Spiritual Science	Animal kingdom
Human moral progress	Humans (Animal-humans) on Jupiter
Beyond Spiritual Science	Jupiter Angelic culture-Angel kingdom
Old Saturn Man in Us—physical	Minerals-atoms-Archai-
	moral intuitions-Spirit Human
Old Sun Man in Us—etheric	Plant kingdom-Archangels-
	moral inspirations-Life-Spirit
Old Moon Man in Us—astral	Animal kingdom-Angels-
	moral imaginations-Spirit-Self
Moral breath of Earthly man	Human kingdom-animal humans
Spiritual Human I Am—ego	Regions of continents-oceans-
	air-warmth-Angelic realm

The chart above should demonstrate that everything you think, feel, or do is creating your future environment and your future body. This is a revelation concerning the workings of karma. What you do now becomes who you will be in the future. Or as the *Bible* tells us.

> "A man reaps what he sows. Whoever sows to please their flesh, from the flesh will reap destruction; whoever sows to please the Spirit, from the Spirit will reap eternal life. Let us not become weary in doing good, for at the proper time we will reap a harvest if we do not give up." (*Galatians* 6:7-9)

Steiner's clarifications on the nature of heaven coincide not only with Christianity but with all traditional religions. The descriptions of the heavenly realms are consistent across religious beliefs. Usually, the descriptions are sketchy and incomplete and the rules for "getting into heaven" are quite different among the various religions, myths, and tales. For the Greeks, all you had to do to get into heaven (the fixed stars) is to drink the god's nectar or eat their ambrosia or even take a bite of a golden apple from the Garden of the Hesperides. You could even be born into heaven by having the divine blood of the gods (ichor) coursing through your veins as a son or daughter of a god or goddess. Even great human labors and feats like those of Psyche and Heracles could earn you a place in the home of the gods. But the Greeks also had their ideas of karma and reincarnation dictating that your deeds in the physical world determine your future "home" in either the starry heavens or the underworld of shadows. This explains why Christ asks His followers to dedicate every thought, feeling, and deed to love in an effort to please God and attain the rewards of heaven:

> "You shall love the Lord your God with all your heart, with all
> your soul, with all your strength, and with all your mind, and your
> neighbor as yourself." (*Luke* 10:27)

It is incumbent upon each individual to take responsibility for karma and build their own heaven through their personal loving thoughts, feelings, and deeds during this incarnation of the Earth so that the Future Jupiter (heaven) will be as beautiful as the description of New Jerusalem in the *Book of Revelation* of Saint John the Divine. Just read the description of St. John's vision of New Jerusalem and you will see that what Dr. Steiner describes in the selections below are in keeping with Biblical wisdom.

In the *Book of Revelation*, after Saint John witnesses the new heaven and a new Earth, an Angel takes him "in the Spirit" to a vantage point on "a great and high mountain" to see New Jerusalem "descend out of heaven." The enormous city comes out of heaven down to the New Earth. John's elaborate description of New Jerusalem retains many features of the Garden of Eden, such as rivers, a square shape, a wall with a gate, and the Tree of Life. New Jerusalem had a great, high wall with twelve gates and with twelve Angels in charge of the gates. There were three gates on each side. The twelve gates were twelve pearls; each gate was made from a single pearl. New Jerusalem is 'pure gold, like clear glass' and its 'brilliance is like a very costly stone, as a stone of crystal-clear jasper.' The streets of the city are also made of 'pure gold, like transparent glass.' The base of the city is laid out in a square and surrounded by a wall made of transparent jasper. The height, length, and width are of equal dimensions—as it was with the Holy of Holies in the Tabernacle and First Temple. God and the Lamb are the city's temple. The river of the Water of Life flows down the middle of the great street of the city from the Throne of God. The tree bears twelve kinds of fruit and yields its fruit every month—'the leaves of the tree were for healing those of all nations.' The city is free of sin and the servants of God will have the power and likeness of God and 'His name will be on their foreheads.' They will 'preach the Eternal Gospel' and sing the 'new song of the lamb.' Night will no longer fall, and the inhabitants of the city will 'have need of no lamp nor light of the Sun, for the Lord God gives them light.' The inhabitants of New Jerusalem know that God is eternal 'and shall reign forever and ever.'

Saint John's description of New Jerusalem is essentially what Rudolf Steiner tells us about Future Jupiter and aligns with the other *Bible* passages we have quoted that tell of heaven, its environment, and its inhabitants. Even Steiner's descriptions of the transformed human body agree with what Christians believe about Angels. There are also many other details about heaven provided that can be found in only a few places other than Steiner's indications. These wisdom insights are consistent with what ancient natural clairvoyants and prophets tell us about the future. The distinction is that Steiner's cosmology is amazingly detailed, extremely consistent, and can be applied to actual spiritual scientific research. These powerful spiritual teachings awaken us to the responsibility that each individual must take their own personal spiritual development in hand for their future's sake and for the sake of all humanity.

The Future Jupiter (Heaven) According to Rudolf Steiner

Occult Science, Rudolf Steiner, *The Present and Future of Cosmic Evolution*, GA 13

"The transformations in the things of the Earth existing outside the human being occur with a certain relationship to humanity's own evolution. After the Seventh Cultural Period has run its course, the Earth will be visited by a catastrophe that may be likened to what occurred between the Atlantean and Post-Atlantean ages, and the transformed Earth conditions after this catastrophe will again evolve in seven time periods. Human souls who will then be incarnated will experience, at a higher stage, the union with the higher world experienced by the Atlanteans at a lower stage. Only those human beings, however, in whom are incarnated souls that have developed in a manner possible through the influences of the Greco-Latin Cultural Period and the subsequent Fifth, Sixth, and Seventh Cultural Periods of the Post-Atlantean evolution will be able to cope with the newly formed Earth conditions. The inner being of such souls will correspond to what the Earth has then become. Other souls will then have to remain behind, whereas previously they would have had the choice of creating the conditions for advancement. Souls who will have created the possibility for themselves, in the transition from the Fifth to the Sixth Post-Atlantean Period, of penetrating supersensible knowledge with the forces of intellect and feeling, will have the maturity for the corresponding conditions following the next great catastrophe. The Fifth and Sixth Post-Atlantean Periods are, so to speak, decisive. In the Seventh, the souls who will have reached the goal of the Sixth will develop correspondingly further; the other souls, however, will, under the changed conditions of the environment, find but little opportunity of retrieving what they have neglected. Only at some future time will conditions appear again that will permit this.

Evolution thus advances from age to age. Supersensible cognition not only observes such future changes in which the Earth alone takes part, but it is also aware of changes that occur in co-operation with the heavenly bodies in its environment. A time will come when the evolution of the Earth and mankind will have advanced so far that the spiritual powers and beings that had to sever themselves from the Earth during the Lemurian Epoch, in order to make possible the continued progress of the Earth's beings, will be able to unite themselves again with the Earth. The Moon will then reunite with the Earth. This will occur because at that time a sufficiently large number of human souls will possess so much inner strength that they will use these Moon forces for the benefit of further evolution. This will occur at a time when, alongside the high level of development that will have been reached by a certain number of human souls, another development will occur that has taken the direction toward evil. The laggard souls will have accumulated in their karma so much error, ugliness, and evil that they will form, for the time being, a special union of evil and aberrant human beings who violently oppose the community of good men.

The good humanity will through its development acquire the use of the Moon forces and thereby so transform the evil part also that, as a special realm of the Earth, it may participate in further evolution. Through this work of the good humanity, the Earth, united with the Moon, will be able, after a certain period of evolution, to reunite also with the Sun and with the other planets. Then, after an intermediate stage, which presents itself as a sojourn in a higher world, the Earth will transform itself into the Future Jupiter. Within this state, what is now called the mineral kingdom will no longer exist; the forces of this mineral kingdom will be transformed into plant forces. The plant kingdom, which in contrast to the present plant kingdom will have an entirely new form, appears during the Future Jupiter state as the lowest kingdom. To this a higher kingdom is added, the transformed animal kingdom; above it there is a human kingdom, which proves to be the progeny of the evil community that arose on the Earth; above all these are to be found the descendants of the good community of Earth men, a human kingdom of a higher order. A great part of the activity of this latter human kingdom consists in the work of ennobling the fallen souls of the evil community, so that they may still be able to find their way back into the actual human kingdom. The Future Venus evolution will be one in which the plant kingdom also will have disappeared; the lowest kingdom at that time will be the retransformed animal kingdom; this will be joined on an ascending scale by three human kingdoms of different degrees of perfection. During the Future Venus state the Earth remains united with the Sun; during the Future Jupiter state, however, evolution proceeds in such a way that at a certain point of time the Sun departs once more from Future Jupiter and the latter receives its effects from the outside. After a time, the union of Sun and Future Jupiter (Jupiter minus the Sun in contradistinction to Jupiter with the Sun) again occurs, and the transformation gradually proceeds over into the Future Venus state. During that state a special cosmic body splits off that contains all the beings who have resisted evolution, a so to speak "irredeemable Moon," which now moves toward an evolution, for the character of which no expression can be found because it is too dissimilar to anything that man can experience on Earth. The evolved mankind, however, advances in a completely spiritualized existence to the Future Vulcan evolution, the description of which does not lie within the scope of this book."

The Foundations of Esotericism, Rudolf Steiner, Lecture IV, September 29, 1905, Berlin, GA 93a

"The consciousness of the beehive, not of the single bee, is immensely lofty. The wisdom of this consciousness will only be attained by man in the Future Venus Incarnation of the Earth. Then, he will have the consciousness which is necessary in order to build with a substance which he creates out of his own being. Through transferring one's consciousness into the beehive, through taking on the Future Venus consciousness, one learns something entirely different from anything else on Earth, the complete recession of the element of sex. With the bees what is sexual is vested only in the one queen. The sexuality (kama) is almost entirely eliminated; the drones are killed. Here we have the prototype of something which will actually be accomplished in a future humanity, when work is the highest principle. It is only through the impulse of the spirit that one gains the faculty of transferring oneself into the community of the bees.

The mineral kingdom in its present state of separation only came into existence during the Fourth Round [Planetary Condition/Globe]. After this, the entire mineral kingdom will be spiritualized by man. He transforms it with the 'plough of his spirit'. Everything that man does today, the entire world of industry, is the transformation of the mineral kingdom. The whole mineral kingdom will be transformed by man. To a great extent this will be brought about by oscillating electricity no longer requiring wires. Here man will be working right into the molecules and atoms. At the end of the Fourth Round, he will have transformed the entire mineral kingdom.

From the Fifth Round [Future Jupiter Planetary Condition] onwards man will do the same with the plant kingdom. He will be able consciously to carry out the process which is now carried out by the plant. As the plant takes in carbonic acid and builds up its body from the carbon so the human being of the Fifth Round will himself create his body out of the materials of his environment. Sex will cease to exist. Man will then himself have to work on his body, will have to produce it for himself. The same process of transforming carbon, which the plant now carries out unconsciously, will then be carried out consciously by man. He will then transform matter just as today the plant transforms the air into carbon. That is true alchemy. Carbon is the Philosopher's Stone. The man of the 18th century who pointed this out was indicating the transformation which is now carried out by the plants, and which later will be carried out by man.

When from the higher planes one studies consciousness as it functions in the beehive, one learns how later man will produce matter out of himself. In the future the human body will also be built up out of carbon; it will then be like a soft diamond. Then one will no longer inhabit the body from within but will have it before one as an external body. Today the planets are built up in this way by the planetary spirits. From a being requiring a body produced by others, man will transform himself into a being who manifests himself through emanation. At that time, he will consist of three members: 'Man in the evening who goes on three', as the Sphinx says. The original four organs have undergone metamorphosis. At first the hands were also organs of movement. Then they became organs for the spiritual. In the future only three organs will remain; the heart as Budhi-organ, the two-petalled lotus-flower between the eyes, and the left hand as the organ of movement. This future state is also related to Blavatsky's indication of a second spinal column. The pineal gland and the pituitary gland organize a second spinal column which later unites itself with the first. The second spinal column will descend in front from the head.

To the front of the head lies the thinking part, above, the part of feeling, to the back of the head that of willing. The esoteric pupil learns to bring these consciously into connection with one another. Later these three parts become completely separated. He must then control the three parts in the same way as an ant heap controls the males, females, and workers."

The Destiny of Individuals and of Nations, Lecture IX, Berlin, March 9, 1915, GA 157

"This is something we would find difficult to do in a natural way whilst on Earth, yet in the course of evolution it will be achieved, though in a less crude fashion than just described. It will be achieved as mankind develops further in the course of Earth evolution and grows towards Future Jupiter [Planetary Condition]. Then his hands, his physical hands, will in fact become immovable. On Future Jupiter human beings will no longer have physical hands that are mobile organs, for they will be fixed. On the other hand, their astral and ether hands will in part be able to move outside those physical hands. Only a trace of the physical hands will be left on Future Jupiter, and they will be immobile; the astral or ether hands on the other hand will be able to move freely, like wings. As a result, Jupiter man will not merely think with his brain, for his fixed hands will enable him to reflect into the elements now united with his physical hands. His thinking will be much more alive, much more all-embracing. When a physical organ comes to rest, the spirit or soul element belonging to it will be liberated and able to develop spiritual and soul activity.

You see, it is the same with the brain. When we were still living on the Old Moon [Planetary Condition], we had organs up here (the cranium) that moved like hands. These organs have become fixed. On the Old Moon we did not yet have a solid cranium; the organs now folded up to form the brain were then able to move like hands. Because of this, men living on the Old Moon were not yet able to think the way men do on Earth. A clairvoyant assessing thought activity clearly perceives that in a human being who is awake the sleeping organs in his brain do indeed move like wings, the way I have described that astral and ether hands would move if our physical hands could be immobilized. It really happened that with the transition from the Old Moon to the Earth state 'hands' were brought under control up here. They are still held fast by the solid skull and because of this the etheric and astral elements are free. Our organs need to be developed further. These hands cannot remain as they are when we develop to the Future Jupiter state—they will undergo a physical change, just as our brain underwent the change that made it an organ of reflection. This is a process we may consider one of natural evolution."

Foundations of Esotericism, Rudolf Steiner, Lecture XXIV, 1905, GA 93a

"Just as now human circumstances conform to fundamental laws of Nature, so in the future will they conform to what is moral."

Planetary	Condition	States of Consciousness
Old Saturn	=	Deep trance-consciousness
Old Sun	=	Dreamless sleep-consciousness
Old Moon	=	Dreaming sleep or picture consciousness
Earth	=	Waking consciousness or awareness of objects
Future Jupiter	=	Psychic or conscious picture-consciousness
Future Venus	=	Super-psychic or conscious life-consciousness
Future Vulcan	=	Spiritual or self-conscious universal consciousness

An Esoteric Cosmology, Rudolf Steiner, Lecture XVII, Paris, 1906, GA 94

"There are seven Mysteries of Life which up until now have never been spoken of outside the ranks of occult brotherhoods. Only in our age is it possible to speak of them openly. They have been called the seven 'inexpressible' or 'unutterable' mysteries. On Earth we attempt to deal with the Fourth Mystery, that of Birth and Death."

These Seven Great Mysteries are as follows:

1. The Mystery of the Abyss (Old Saturn) [a]

2. The Mystery of Number (Old Sun) [b]

3. The Mystery of Alchemy (Old Moon) [c]

4. The Mystery of Birth and Death (Present Earth) [d]

5. The Mystery of Evil (Future Jupiter) [e]

6. The Mystery of the Word, of the Logos (Future Venus) [f]

7. The Mystery of Divine Bliss (Future Vulcan) [g]

The first public mention of the "Seven Great Mysteries", or "Seven Unutterable Secrets" was by H. P. Blavatsky in 1888 wherein she stated in *The Secret Doctrine*, Vol. I, by H.P. Blavatsky, (London, 1888; pg. 42):

"Out of the "Seven Truths" and Revelations, or rather revealed secrets, four only have been handed to us, as we are still in the Fourth Round, and the world also has had only four Buddhas, so far. This is a very complicated question, and will receive more ample treatment later on.

So far "there are only Four Truths, and Four Vedas"- say the Buddhists and Hindus. For a similar reason Irenæus insisted on the necessity of Four Gospels. But as every new Root-Race at the head of a Round must have its revelation and revealers, the next Round will bring the Fifth, the following the Sixth, and so on."

In the *Occult Movements in the 19th Century* lecture cycle given in Dornach from the 10th to the 25th of October, 1915 (GA 254) Rudolf Steiner makes frequent reference to the High Church Anglican and independent Rosicrucian author C.G. Harrison; who has provided extensive commentaries on: *The Secret Doctrine*, by H.P. Blavatsky in his book: *The Transcendental Universe; Six Lectures on Occult Science, Theosophy, and the Catholic Faith*, (London 1893; pg. 131); therein C.G. Harrison gives the following designations for the Seven Great Mysteries:

1. Abyss. 2. Number. 3 Affinity. 4. Birth and Death. 5. Evil.
6. The Word. 7. Godliness.

[a] Before the Old Saturn Planetary Condition nothing of mankind's prototype-vehicles had yet come into existence. Hence the Mystery of the Abyss refers to the "creation from nothingness"; whereby by the Thrones (Spirits of Will) donated the initial warmth at the beginning of the Old Saturn Planetary Condition to serve as the initial prototype for what would subsequently evolve into the human physical bodies on the 4th Planetary Condition, our present Earth; with the core of this initial impulse being the warmth of the blood that carries the 4th Principle, the Human Ego or "I Am".

[b] Some of this Mystery can be studied in Pythagorean philosophy of numbers.

[c] C.G. Harrison in *The Transcendental Universe*, referred to above, as the "Mystery of Affinity", as it is in reference to the properties of attraction and repulsion that are an inherent characteristic of the astral world. We can learn something of this Mystery through the works of Paracelsus and Jacob Boehme.

[d] The present Earth Planetary Condition brings us to the experience of both Birth and Death, with the ultimate result of the continuity of consciousness being separated into intervals of consciousness and unconsciousness between incarnations, and similar disruptions of the continuity of consciousness in sleep. Please note: There is no recapitulation of any 4th Stage of a 7-fold cycle.

[e] Reference is made to this in the *Apocalypse of St. John*. This 5th Mystery recapitulates the 3rd Mystery of Affinity on a higher state of being.

[f] This 6th Mystery is also connected to the Music of the Spheres, and recapitulates the 2nd Mystery of Number on a higher state of being.

[g] This 7th Mystery is the most occult; it recapitulates the 1st Mystery of the Abyss on a higher state of being.

Art as Seen in the Light of Mystery Wisdom, Rudolf Steiner, Lecture VII, *Future Jupiter and its Beings*, Dornach, January 3, 1915, GA 275

"I will confess that I would never have understood the part about the Elohim breathing the living being of man into his mouth and nose, if I had not known beforehand that the breath of Earthly human beings also contains the first germinal beginnings of the beings who will become human on Jupiter. But Jupiter human beings can only arise from the kind of breath that owes its existence to deeds that obey the 'you shall', and which are therefore moral actions.

Thus, we see that through our Earthly morality we take a creative part in the whole cosmic order. It is indeed a creative power, and we can see that Spiritual Science gives us a strong impulse for moral action by telling us that we are working against the creation of Jupiter human beings, if we do not act in a moral way on Earth. This gives morality a very real value and makes its existence worthwhile.

So, we see that our Earth evolution contains two tendencies: good deeds that contain the impulse to work creatively on Earth in preparation for Jupiter, so that man's successor on the human level can come into being. But evil deeds have also brought into our evolution the tendency to drag the Earth back again to the Old Moon period and make it dependent on everything to do with the subconscious."

Heaven and Earth Will Pass Away But My Words Will Not Pass Away, Rudolf Steiner, Dornach, June 3, 1915, GA 162

"But the Earth will pass through another evolutionary period in the future. Then will the intuitions of the Spirits of Personality become more and more densified. In our own Age they still are extremely attenuated forms, but as we progress from the 5th to the 6th and 7th Earth Epochs these intuitions become denser. The Earth will pass away, but these intuitions are preserved within the Spirits of Personality. But when [Future] Jupiter begins to exist, these Spirits of Personality advance to the rank of Spirits of Form, and the impulses they have learned to form during the Earth-Age [Planetary Condition/Globe] now become actual forms; and because they are Saturn forms, they will be mineral.

Thus, at the end of the Earth Planetary Condition these intuitions become densified cosmic impulses and later, forms. And when they become forms upon [the Future] Jupiter [Planetary Condition], they constitute the mineral foundation of [Future] Jupiter. During the second evolutionary half period of the Earth, the Spirits of Personality continuously work there—penetrate—into our Saturn man; they win for themselves the impulses which they then ray forth into the world; and these again send out forms, but these forms are the [Future]Jupiter [Planetary Condition]; Jupiter will be constituted of nothing but these forms. We have in us the Saturn man [Old Saturn], but as this Saturn man is in close connection with the activity of the Spirits of Personality, he is the germ for [Future] Jupiter [Planetary Condition]. [Future] Jupiter will obtain all his mineral foundation from the Saturn man we carry in us.

So now you have obtained a glimpse of the Spirits of Personality and their task during Earth evolution. And you will realize that this is the fact, we, by means of everything we may develop in this direction will be able to evolve a mineral [Future] Jupiter [Planetary Condition]. But this mineral [Future] Jupiter will take shape under any circumstances. That is definitely provided for, and is a certainty, in the further evolution of the Cosmos. But consider that this [Future] Jupiter possesses as yet nothing equivalent to our plants, animals and human beings; we ourselves—as mankind—would find it impossible to exist upon such a Jupiter; for the hidden Saturn man within us is transformed into this Jupiter [condition]—because this Saturn man in his deep sleep, dreams what the Earth man consciously imagines.

You see, under these conditions the Sun man [Old Sun] could bring it to nothing actual in us. The Archangels would realize only inspirations; and were things to proceed as they have so far been described, a mineral [Future] Jupiter would arise and over and around it would flow inspirations— densified, certainly, but they would merely pass over [Future] Jupiter. In order that some equivalent to our vegetable kingdom shall come into existence, something additional is necessary, we must evolve something else beyond the Earth man. And this is nothing else than something that Earthly man can never again experience with his physical body: it is what we can imbibe from Spiritual Science. Hence, I propose to call this man the Spiritual-Scientific Man [Spirit-Self], despite its strange sound, who aspires to and reaches out for things that extend far beyond the Earth.

With all that we absorb from Spiritual Science, the Sun man [Old Sun] in us can really do something. He can transmute his dim, sleeping, vegetable-like sensations and conceptions into inspirations, which will become more and more densified during the remainder of the Earth Period [Planetary Condition]; and these will ensure, that not only indefinite sphere harmony shall enclose [Future] Jupiter; but that this harmony of the spheres definitely becomes growth of vegetation, as this took place also in the case of Earthly plants: they are created by the Harmony of the Spheres and drawn out by light.

We therefore come to this conclusion: If the development which the Earth itself has so far achieved, and which does not lead to the Spiritual-Scientific man, were alone to permeate the world in the future, there could arise only a mineral Jupiter in the Cosmos. Toward this end all materialistic world conceptions are aiming. Materialists hate the very idea that [Future] Jupiter should produce a vegetable kingdom; in the depths of their souls they ask nothing better than that [Future] Jupiter [Planetary Condition] be constructed of minerals only. If today we search through materialistic science, laboratories, etc., we shall find that everything is working in the direction of a mineral Jupiter [Planetary Condition]. And without Spiritual Science this would merely prove to be a dead slagheap, quite incapable of sustaining growth of plants.

The task of the (present) Beings of the hierarchy of Archangel on [Future] Jupiter—the production of the equivalent of our vegetable kingdom—is prepared by us when we raise ourselves to the stage of Spiritual Science. We may therefore say: The experiences of the sleeping Sun man, mature at the end of the Earth Period [Planetary Condition], so as to furnish cosmic impulses for the Jupiterian plant world through the Archangels.

And so, we will not try and become conscious of the aim of Spiritual Science; we will learn to know that our Spiritual Science really does give the Hierarchy of the Archangels the possibility of endowing [Future] Jupiter [Planetary Condition] with a cover of vegetation. What the Sun man experiences through the concepts of Spiritual Science can be used by the Archangels in the development of vegetation upon Jupiter.

It will be something which the dreamer in man, the Moon man, will dream in a tremendously more intensive manner than the Sun man today can experience of the conceptions of Spiritual Science in his sleep. But the experiences of the dreamer in a future age will be grasped and reformed by the Beings of the Angels and carried by them to the [Future] Jupiter [Planetary Condition], to further enrich Jupiter by adding, upon the mineral and vegetable foundation, another kingdom, the equivalent of the animals. And we say: The dream conceptions of the Moon man (or the dreamer in man) becomes for Jupiter condensed imaginations, foundation of an animal kingdom through the Angels.

And finally, something further will appear during the evolution of the Earth. We look forward to a future where we can sense something very wonderful. That which will then come to pass will produce the germ which will enable the human being of the Earth himself to erect his kingdom upon the [Future] Jupiter [Planetary Condition], and it will be something entirely new.

Thus, all that today can be developed with the help of the Earthly man will progress further, and then, after the ages during which something new will have continually been developed, will arise something which this Earth man can now conceive as the highest flower, the apex of the Spiritual evolution of the Earth. And out of this conception will be born the power by which Earth man upon [Future] Jupiter can continue his progress through himself. Thus, we can say: The conceptions of Earth man become impulses— through the Soul-contents of the most evolved of humanity—for the evolution of humanity upon the [Future] Jupiter [Planetary Condition].

Our Spirits of Personality will then have advanced to the Spirits of Form; our Archangels to Spirits of Personality; our Angels to Archangels; man will have risen to the ranks of the Angels. Then it will be possible for man, by means of the highest and purest conceptions of Earth man, in the Hierarchy of the Jupiter-Angels (which mankind will then constitute) to continue his Jupiterean Spiritual development. His possession in the form of evolutionary progress will then be similar to those possessed by man at the end of the Atlantean Epoch to enable them to inaugurate the true evolution of the Earth.

Well, from the stones of Earth, from the plants and animals of Earth—in short—from the physical bodies of the Earth—nothing new can evolve,— they are there in order to be discarded—but from the Saturn man in you the mineral Jupiter comes into existence. So true is this, as it is true that in the fowl that runs out of your way nothing exists of this parent fowl but a tiny germ within the egg—so nothing exists upon the Earth as a basis for the future Jupiter than the Saturn germs that live in the human body. That is all that will pass intact through the pralaya [period of Cosmic rest] to the [Future] Jupiter [Planetary Condition]; all the rest is discarded—falls away from the physical Earth. (I am now referring to the physical Earth, not to souls). And should anyone harbor the notion that the physical Earth will become transformed, he holds a nebulous idea; for the concrete fact is that everything is dispersed into the Cosmos, with the exception of all the Saturn seeds, which are absorbed by the Archai, to be transmuted into the atoms intended to form the mineral atoms on [Future] Jupiter. We must think of these atoms as the most inner essence of the Moon man, i.e., the man on the Old Moon—but used by those Beings who were in advance of man in evolution, who transmuted this very central part of the Moon man to an Earth atom. Today this resides no longer in the Saturn man, but in the Earth.

This is the atom in its reality, compared with which the physicist's atom is a very childish concept. For this atom, in actual fact, has come into being in a most complicated manner. Think for a moment that this atom must evolve from that which man has developed upon Saturn, and which he has preserved during the Sun, Moon, and Earth Planetary Conditions, and that later is to be changed to an atom for [Future] Jupiter by the Spirits of Personality, who, upon Jupiter, will hold the rank of Spirits of Form. Thus, is the world complicated.

When we think that all the spiritual culture that men can attain here will form the inner foundation of [Future] Jupiter; that the endeavors of our Spiritual Science will form the future vegetable kingdom upon Jupiter; and that future (and further) progress will be the seed of the animal kingdom on Jupiter, and, finally, seriously ponder over the truth that within the Saturn man in us lies the germ for the physical shell of Jupiter, that in our Sun man resides that which we must convert into the Jupiterean vegetation, again the Moon man holds potencies that will be transformed into the animal kingdom of Jupiter—and that everything belonging to the Earth—including the stars, will cease to be—will enter into pralaya [period of Cosmic rest]—when we ponder over these marvels, we become a pupil of Him who said: "Heaven and Earth will pass away but my words will not pass away."

Everything else there is to man will be lost, dissolving into the Universe once the Earth has reached its goal. The minerals, plants, and animals around us will pass away. Only the Saturn man you have been remains, in the form of fine dust particles. It will go over from Earth to [Future] Jupiter existence, forming the solid skeleton of Jupiter. Those are real atoms for Jupiter. People studying external science today, people thinking in an external way, influence their Saturn man to the effect that they produce atoms for Jupiter in their Saturn man. That is how Jupiter gets its atoms. What we are able to take across to Jupiter through the Saturn man in us merely causes Jupiter to be a mineral sphere. Plants could not grow on it. If plants are to grow on Jupiter, the Sun man in us must also be given something. This Sun man in us only receives something from now on and into the future if men and women absorb concepts developed in Spiritual Science; for the concepts we absorb outside, from external science, enter into Saturn man. What we absorb by way of thoughts engendered through Spiritual Science enters into the Sun man. This is why Spiritual Science calls for greater activity. Its thoughts differ from those of external science in that they are active. They have to be grasped in a living way and it is impossible to remain passive towards thinking activity the way we do in the external world. In Spiritual Science everything has to be actively thought out, we have to be inwardly active. This has an effect on the Sun man in us. And if there were no Sun Principle in man, the Jupiter of the future would be entirely mineral, with no plant world. People going through spiritual development take something across that will give rise to a plant world on Jupiter. Through the Sun principle in us we take across the future plant world. All we have to do to make Jupiter barren is reject Spiritual Science. We can establish Spiritual Science now in order that there shall be vegetation on Jupiter.

A time will come, however, when it will be necessary for us to try and influence the dreamer in us just as we influence the Sun man, and the whole of our external science influences Saturn man. Jupiter as mineral mass will be based on what external science makes of Saturn man. Its vegetation will be based on what Spiritual Science makes of Sun man. Animal life on Jupiter will arise from something that is going to follow on after Spiritual Science. It will be based on the Spiritual Science of the future. Then something else will follow which will influence man on [Future] Jupiter, something which is still to come. It will provide the basis for Jupiter culture in the real sense.

At present, therefore, we are in a period in life where we prepare the mineral nucleus of Jupiter through external science and where Spiritual Science influences its plant life, providing the basis for vegetation on Jupiter. The future will bring the principle that influences the dreamer, and this will provide the basis for animal life on Jupiter. Only after this will come the principle which corresponds to what man is today producing in his thinking, feeling and will activity. This is guided by higher wisdom to the effect that when Earth evolution has come to an end man will be able to take himself, as man, across to Jupiter.

This is how we are involved in the evolution of the Earth, and we perceive, out of our very own human nature, that we are part of the "Great World", of the macrocosm. We know that everything we do is of account. We know that joining in the pursuit of Spiritual Science we contribute to vegetative life for [Future] Jupiter and that through the things we put in words we create what will be given to the future at the Jupiter stage of the world.

Just think, dear friends, as I have told you, everything belonging to the mineral kingdom will disperse in the world; everything belonging to the plant kingdom will disperse; everything belonging to the animal kingdom will disperse. Nothing will continue on from the Earth except for the mineral atoms coming from man, from the Saturn parts of human beings. Nothing of the mineral, plant and animal worlds passes across to [Future] Jupiter. The only thing which will continue is the Saturn man now within us. This will be the mineral kingdom on [Future] Jupiter.

Let us imagine ourselves on [Future] Jupiter. What are the atoms of [Future] Jupiter? They are the Saturn parts of present-day man. It is a nonsense to talk of atoms of the kind modern physicists' speak of. Everything man gains from the whole of the Earth enters into Saturn man and later becomes [Future] Jupiter atoms.

Words coming from external science influence Saturn man and become the atoms of [Future] Jupiter. Words coming from Spiritual Science and influencing Sun man pass across to form the vegetation on [Future] Jupiter. That which acts on the dreamer passes across to form the animal kingdom on [Future] Jupiter. The moral progress made by man and what he gains through words of the Spiritual Science of the future—that will be man on [Future] Jupiter. It will be words, wisdom of thoughts. This shall endure."

The Foundations of Esotericism, Rudolf Steiner, Lecture IX, Berlin, Oct 4, 1905, GA 93a

"In times to come man will bring forth into his surroundings what he feels. This will be imparted to the fluid element. The entire fluid element of the planet which will follow next [Future] Jupiter will be an expression of what people feel. Today man sends out words; they are inscribed into the Akasha. There they remain, even though the airwaves vanish. Out of these words the [Future] Jupiter will later be formed. When therefore today man uses evil, blasphemous language, then on [Future] Jupiter terrible formations will be brought about. This is why one should be so very careful of what one says, and why it is so immensely important that man should be master of his speech. In the future man will also send out his feelings; the conditions of the fluids on [Future] Jupiter will be a result of feelings on the Earth. What man speaks today will give [Future] Jupiter its form; what he feels will engender its inner warmth; what he wills determines the separate beings inhabiting [Future] Jupiter. The [Future] Jupiter will be constructed out of the basic powers of the human soul.

Just as today we can trace the rock formation of the Earth back to earlier conditions, so will the rock formation of the [Future] Jupiter be the result of our words. The ocean of [Future] Jupiter, the warmth of [Future] Jupiter, will arise out of the feelings of present-day humanity. The beings of [Future] Jupiter will arise out of human will. Thus, the inhabitants of a previous planet create the basic conditions for its successor. And beings who today still [gap in text ...] hover over the Earth, as was once the case with the Monads, will enter into incarnation on the [Future] Jupiter. There will then exist a kind of Jupiter-Lemurian race. Beings will be there which we have created as the Pitris [lunar Angels] did. Just as we inhabited the grotesque forms of the [Old] Moon, so these beings will inhabit the forms which we develop by means of our pineal gland."

Occult Science—An Outline, Chapter VI, *Present and Future Evolution of the World and of Mankind*, Rudolf Steiner, GA 13

"To a stage of seership higher than is needed for gaining knowledge of [Old] Moon and of the [Future] Jupiter, beings and entities become perceptible which are the further-developed forms of what was present during [Old] Sun evolution. They are now at such a lofty level of existence as to elude a power of perception whose range is limited to the [Old] Moon and to the forms deriving from it. Also, the spiritual picture of this higher world divides on further contemplation into two. The one part leads to a knowledge of the past [Old] Sun evolution; the other manifests a future cosmic form of the Earth, namely the form into which it will have changed when the results of all that has taken place on Earth and on [Future] Jupiter have flowed into the forms of yonder world—the forms deriving from the past [Old] Sun-condition. In the language of Spiritual Science, in the future Universe a higher stage of consciousness is thus enabled to perceive what may be designated as the [Future] Venus state. Lastly, a supersensible consciousness even more highly developed perceives an evolutionary state of the more distant future to which the name of [Future] Vulcan may be given. [Future] Vulcan is in like relation to [Old] Saturn evolution as [Future] Venus to [Old]Sun and [Future] Jupiter to [Old]Moon. Thus, in considering the past, the present and the future of Earth evolution we have to name its successive stages: [Old]Saturn, [Old] Sun, [Old] Moon, Earth, [Future] Jupiter, [Future] Venus, and [Future] Vulcan.

After a cosmic interval—a sojourn in a higher world [pralaya/cosmic rest]—the Earth will then be transmuted into the [Future] Jupiter condition. In [Future] Jupiter, what we now call the mineral kingdom will exist no longer; the forces of this kingdom will have been changed into plant-like forces. Thus, upon [Future] Jupiter the vegetable kingdom, though in a very different form, will be the lowest. Above it will be the animal kingdom, likewise considerably altered, and then a human kingdom, recognizable as the spiritual descendants of the bad humanity originating upon Earth. Lastly, the descendants of the good humanity will constitute a human kingdom on a higher level. This is the human kingdom proper, and a great part of its work will be to influence and ennoble the souls who have fallen into the other group, so that they may yet gain entrance to it.

In the [Future] Venus [Planetary Condition], the plant kingdom too will have disappeared. The lowest will then be the animal kingdom, metamorphosed a second time. Above it will be three human kingdoms, differing in degrees of perfection. During the [Future] Venus [Planetary Condition], the Earth will remain united with the Sun. In the [Future] Jupiter evolution [Planetary Condition], on the other hand, there will come a time when the Sun will separate again and [Future] Jupiter will be receiving Solar influences from without. Then, after Sun and [Future] Jupiter have again become united, the transition to the [Future] Venus state [Planetary Condition] will gradually be accomplished. From [Future] Venus, at a certain stage, a separate celestial body becomes detached. This is, as it were, an "irreclaimable Moon"—it includes all the beings who have persisted in withstanding the true course of evolution. It enters now upon a line of development such as no words can portray, so utterly unlike is it to anything within the range of man's experience on Earth. The evolved humanity on the other hand, in a form of existence utterly spiritualized, goes forward into [Future] Vulcan evolution, any description of which would be beyond the compass of this book.

Now, from the Spirits of Form, man receives his independent I, his Ego. And in the future the I of man will harmonize with the beings of Earth, [Future] Jupiter, [Future] Venus, and [Future] Vulcan by virtue of the new force which Earthly evolution is implanting in the pristine Wisdom. It is the power of Love. In man on Earth, it has to have its beginning.

The Cosmos of Wisdom is thus evolving into a Cosmos of Love. All that the I of man brings to development within him will grow into Love. It is the sublime Sun Being, of whom we had to tell when describing the evolution of the Christ-Event, who at His revelation stands forth as the all-embracing prototype of Love. Into the innermost depth of man's being the seed of Love is thereby planted. Thence it shall grow and spread until it fills the whole of cosmic evolution. Even as the pristine Wisdom now reveals its presence in all the forces of Nature, in all the sense-perceptible outer world upon Earth, so in the future will Love be revealed—Love as a new force of Nature, living in all the phenomena which man will have around him. This is the secret of all future evolution. The knowledge man acquires, and also every deed man does with true understanding, is like the sowing of the seed that will eventually ripen into Love. Only in as much as Love arises in mankind, is true creative work being done for the cosmic future. For it is Love itself which will grow into the potent forces leading mankind on towards the final goal—the goal of spiritualization."

The Apocalypse of St. John, Rudolf Steiner, Lecture IX, June 26, 1908, GA 104

"Today man works upon his soul; in this way he makes his body more and more like the soul, and when the Earth has arrived at the end of its mission his body will have become an outward image of the soul which has taken Christ into itself. Such a man will survive and implant in the next embodiment of our Earth the forces he has thus developed. The [Future] Jupiter will have an appearance such as men are able to bring about by constructing it out of their own bodies. This [Future] Jupiter will, to begin with, receive its form from that which man has made for himself. Imagine that all the bodies you have fashioned are united in a single Cosmic Globe; that will be [Future] Jupiter. In your soul you have the germs of the future form of Jupiter, and of the forces it will contain. And out of [Future] Jupiter will be born the [Future] Jupiter beings. Thus, man is now preparing for the birth of the [Future] Jupiter bodies.

Hence the body is described as that which envelops the soul, which clothes the "I," which is inhabited by the "I," as the temple of the selfhood within, the temple of the Divinity dwelling in man, the Temple of God. When, therefore, you form this body, you are building a future temple, that is to say, the new incarnation of the Earth. You build up [Future] Jupiter in the right way by shaping the human body in the right way. Hence the initiate is commissioned to examine this temple which man will then have built. When this temple of God is measured it will be made manifest whether the soul has done what is right."

The Apocalypse of St. John, Rudolf Steiner, Lecture XII, 1908, GA 104

"We know that the Earth will be followed by its next incarnation, by [Future] Jupiter. When man has reached [Future] Jupiter, he will appear as a different being. The [Future] Jupiter-man will have thoroughly worked from his "I" upon his astral body; and when today we say, the Earth-man who stands before us in the waking condition has developed physical body, etheric body, astral body and "I," we must say of the [Future] Jupiter-man: he will have developed physical body, etheric body, astral body and "I" but he will have changed his astral body into Spirit-Self. He will live at a higher stage of consciousness, a stage which may be described as follows: The ancient dim-picture-consciousness of the [Old] Moon [Planetary Condition], which existed also in the first Epochs of the Earth-consciousness, will again be there with its pictures as clairvoyant consciousness, but it will be furnished with the human "I," so that with this [Future] Jupiter-consciousness man will reflect as logically as he does now with his day-consciousness on the Earth.

The [Future] Jupiter-man therefore will possess spiritual vision of a certain degree. Part of the soul-world will lie open to him; he will perceive the pleasure and pain of those around him in pictures which will arise in his imaginative consciousness. He will therefore live under entirely different moral conditions. Now imagine that as a [Future] Jupiter-man you have a human soul before you. The pain and pleasure of this soul will arise in pictures before you. The pictures of the pain of the other soul will distress you, and if you do not remove the other's pain it will be impossible for you to feel happy. The pictures of sorrow and suffering would torment the [Future] Jupiter-man with his exalted consciousness if he were to do nothing to alleviate this sorrow and thus at the same time remove his own distressing pictures which are nothing but the expression of the sorrow around him. It will not be possible for one to feel pleasure or pain without others also feeling it.

Those who reach the goal of the Earth evolution [Planetary Condition] will then have an astral body completely permeated by the "I," and by the spiritual content which it will have formed. They will have this consciousness as a result, as a fruit of the Earth evolution [Planetary Condition] and will carry it over into the [Future] Jupiter evolution [Planetary Condition]. We might say that when the Earth period [Planetary Condition] has thus come to an end man will have gained capacities which are symbolically represented by the building of the New Jerusalem. Man will then already look into that picture-world of [Future] Jupiter; the Spirit-Self will then be fully developed in him. That is the goal of the Earth evolution. What, then, is man to gain in the course of his Earthly evolution? What is the first goal? The transformation of the astral body. This astral body, which today is always free of the physical and etheric bodies at night, will appear in the future as a transformed portion of the human being. Man brings into it what he gains on the Earth; but this would not be sufficient for the Earth evolution. Imagine that man were to come out of the physical body and etheric body every night and were to fill his astral body with what he had acquired during the day, but that the physical and etheric bodies were untouched by it. Man would then still not reach his Earthly goal. Something else must take place; it must be possible for man during his Earthly evolution to imprint, at least in the etheric body, what he has taken into himself. It is necessary for this etheric body also to receive effects from what man develops in his astral body.

Man cannot yet of himself work into this etheric body. Upon the [Future] Jupiter [Planetary Condition], when he has transformed his astral body, he will be able to work into this etheric body also, but today he cannot do this; he still needs helpers, so to speak. Upon the [Future] Jupiter he will be capable of beginning the real work on the etheric body. Upon the [Future] Venus he will work upon the physical body; this is the part most difficult to overcome. Today he still has to leave both the physical and etheric bodies every night and emerge from them. But in order that the etheric body may receive its effects, so that man shall gradually learn to work into it, he needs a helper. And the helper who makes this possible is none other than Christ, while we designate the Being who helps man to work into the physical body as the Father. But man cannot work into his physical body before the helper comes who makes it possible to work into the etheric body. "No man cometh to the Father, but by me." No one acquires the capacity of working into the physical body who has not gone through the Christ-Principle. However, when he has reached the goal of Earthly evolution, man will have the capacity—through being able to transform his astral body by his own power—to work upon the etheric body also. This he owes to the living presence of the Christ-Principle on the Earth.

Had Christ not united himself with the Earth as a living being, had he not come into the aura of the Earth, that which is developed in the astral body would not be communicated to the etheric body. From this we see that one who shuts himself up by turning away from the Christ-Principle deprives himself of the possibility of working into his etheric body in the way that is necessary during Earthly evolution.

This second death passes unnoticed over those who have made their etheric body harmonize with the astral body through the reception of the Christ-Principle. The second death has no power over them. But the others feel the second death when they have to pass over into the future astral form. The condition of humanity will then be such that those who have reached the goal of evolution will have entirely permeated their astral body with Christ. They will be ready to pass over to the [Future] Jupiter [Planetary Condition]. Upon our Earth they have made the plan of the [Future] Jupiter evolution [Planetary Condition]. This is the plan which is called the New Jerusalem. They live in a new heaven and a new Earth, that is, [Future] Jupiter. This new [Future] Jupiter will be accompanied by a satellite, composed of those who are excluded from the life in the spiritual, who have experienced the second death and are, therefore, unable to attain the [Future] Jupiter consciousness.

Thus, we have such men as have pressed forward to the [Future] Jupiter consciousness, who have attained to Spirit-Self; and such beings as have thrust away the forces which would have given them this consciousness. They are those who only upon [Future] Jupiter have attained to the "I-consciousness" of the Earth, who exist there, so to speak, as man now exists on the Earth with his four members. But such a man can develop himself only on the Earth, the Earth alone has the environment, the ground, the air, the clouds, the plants, the minerals which are necessary to man if he wishes to gain what may be gained within the four members. [Future] Jupiter will be quite differently formed, it will be a new Earth, the soil, air, water, everything will be different. It will be impossible for beings who have only gained the Earth consciousness to live a normal life; they will be backward beings.

But now comes something more for our comfort. Even on [Future] Jupiter [Planetary Condition] there is still a last possibility, through the strong powers which the advanced will have, to move those fallen beings to turn back and even to convert a number. Only with the [Future] Venus incarnation of the Earth [Planetary Condition] will come the last decision, the unalterable decision."

Cosmosophy, Rudolf Steiner, Volume 1, Lecture VIII, October 9, 1921, GA 207

"All that is woven in this way in the Cosmos out of human etheric bodies, however, becomes in the Cosmos forces of a Future Jupiter realm of nature—a plant-animal, an animal-plant realm. What we observe offers us a guarantee that the human etheric body is the seed of this future realm, a realm that has its place between the world of the plants and that of the animals.

Imagine the mineral world, in which the plant world is immersed, participating in life—not just lying there as dead Earth conveying its substances to the plants through the roots and through the air. Imagine that what the plant has immersed itself in possesses life: an entire living Earth, with no dead mineral realm, and a plant world that is not merely able to immerse life into the mineral realm but is itself alive within a living mineral realm. Imagine this living mineral realm, a future stage in the metamorphosis of our Earth—called in my *Outline of Occult Science* the [Future] Jupiter Stage [Planetary Condition]—a living mineral realm living in such a way that it forms itself into plants, which now immerses itself into the plant realm in a merely material way as chemical processes will be living chemical processes, so that the plant life and the mineral shape are all one. It is this that, as future plant realm, has its seed today in the human physical body. The human physical body today is the seed of a future realm, a future realm of nature.

The Cosmos thus absorbs our etheric body, as if dissolving it into the infinite. All that is woven in this way in the Cosmos out of human etheric bodies, however, becomes in the Cosmos forces of a [Future] Jupiter realm of nature—a plant-animal, an animal-plant realm. What we observe offers us a guarantee that the human etheric body is the seed of this future realm, a realm that has its place between the world of plants and that of animals.

We picture to ourselves the plant world of today, which develops only life; it does not develop sensation. We picture, however, that in a substance resembling that of the present plant world but permeated by a capacity for sensation, an animal-plant realm, a plant-animal realm, develops, which will weave around the future Earth, as it were, or the [Future] Jupiter planet [Planetary Condition]. The sensation will not be identical with the sensation of our present animals, which is confined to the perception of the Earthly;

this sensation will be a cosmic sensation, a perception of the processes surrounding [Future] Jupiter.

On the other hand, out of what apparently is dissolved entirely into the Earthly forces, out of the human physical bodies, there will arise as seed a future world planet with its lowest realm being a mineral-plant realm. Out of what is as though dispersed after death, a second realm of this future world planet will be consolidated, an animal-plant realm, which will weave around it like a kind of living etheric activity.

If we make the description given in *Theosophy* truly living, we at once have something that in its essential nature bursts through its cocoon as seed for the future. It loosens itself from the human being, however, just as the other members of human nature are loosened from him. The physical body loosens itself to become the seed for a plant-mineral realm; the etheric body loosens itself to become the seed for an animal-plant realm. The human astral body is drawn up, as it were, by the universal world environment and becomes the seed for a human-animal realm, for a realm that raises the higher animal nature that exists today to a stage above, where the animal will not move merely in sensation, as it does today, but in thoughts, even in a certain way carrying out reasonable actions, although in a more automatic way than is the case with the present-day human being. This human-animal realm is to be pictured as one in which reasonable actions are carried out that are filled with activity from within and work outward; these actions will not, however, take the same course as those of the present-day human being, in which the reasonable action comes from the center of his I-being. Their actions will not be like that; they will have a more automatic character but will not be the same as the actions of the present animal realm, proceeding merely from instinct. They will be actions carried out by the animal, actions filled with powerful [Future] Jupiter-reason, and the single animal will be placed within this Jupiter-reason.

We now come to the human realm as such. Follow once more in my *Theosophy* how the human realm, after having shed the astral body, rises into the world of spirit and in the world of spirit has inner experiences that can be described there in such a way that the descriptions are pictures of a spiritual outer world. To be able to describe this at all, I have related how in the land of spirit something will be experienced vividly like a continental region of the land of spirit, something like an oceanic region, something like a region of air. In all that is described there in this land of spirit you have pictures of a world that does not exist for the Earthly today. The present Earthly environment is different. Nevertheless, if we wish to describe how things actually are, this must be done by relying upon the larger, outer connections of the Earthly planet—by applying to what we find in the land of spirit all that we connect with our continental regions here and doing the same in the case of the oceanic regions. What is described as continent there, as oceanic region, as air region, as region of warmth, is seen to be permeated at the same time by what the human being carries through the portal of death as moral quality. The moral-spiritual world is described as having directly within it the outwardly substantial, the moral element there being a kind of shadowy outline that does not, however, reach the point of creating a heavenly body, a planet. What the human I lives through there, however, is the seed of these new distributions of categories, of these overall connections, on the planet of [Future] Jupiter. In the human I today, therefore, we have the seed of what will be the overall distribution, the common life in regions that will then look different but that will be looked upon similarly to the way we look upon the regions of continents, oceans, and so on, today.

In this weaving in the land of spirit that I have described in my book, *Theosophy*, we see at once that we are not dealing with the individual human being; in the second region, the oceanic region, we already find human beings together in human relationships, groups of human beings together; something superhuman arises. The I is lifted higher. The I joins with other I's in human groups. Read about this in my description of the land of spirit; it is something that can be described only as a realm standing above the human realm. Into such a realm the human being will enter during the Jupiter existence. It cannot be described, for instance, by my saying that it is an Angel-human realm, for that would not be quite appropriate here, because when I characterize the Angels that is a concept for the present time, which is characterized by the fact that the Angels went through their human stage during the Old Moon evolution. If I therefore wish to characterize what will develop during the future existence of the Earth, or the [Future] Jupiter existence, I must speak in this way: the human being is lifted to a higher sphere; the human being in his outer manifestation, in his bodily manifestation, has developed in such a way that what today lives deep within him, only in his soul, then manifests outwardly. In the future his inner nature—whether he is good or bad—will be revealed in his outer configuration. Today we can gather only through suggestions of the human form whether a person is pedantic, irritable, cruel, or gluttonous. Certain moral qualities are expressed slightly in the physiognomy today, in a person's walk or in some outer form, but always in such a way that they can be denied, that one can plead that it is not one's fault if one has been given lips or jaws suggesting gluttony. Arguing away this outer appearance of the soul element will be absolutely impossible in the future. People who cling to what is material will show it clearly in their form, they will take on Ahrimanic forms. There will be a clear distinction in the future between ahrimanic forms and luciferic forms. A good number of those belonging to various theosophical societies, for instance, are preparing luciferic forms, always dreaming away in the higher regions. There will also be forms, however, that will strike the balance. The dreamy mystics, they will take on luciferic forms; all that will be attempted through the indwelling of Christ, however, is the balance. In short, in the unfolding of what today is I-seed we will have the soul-human realm.

Seed	Unfolding
Human physical body	Plant-mineral realm
Human etheric body	Animal-plant realm
Human astral body	Human-animal realm
Human I	Soul-human realm

Our bond with the Mystery of Golgotha gives us the forces that make Christ the Gardener within us. He will not allow the seeds to deteriorate but will guide them over into a future world. When the mineral realm of the Earth melts away, when the plant realm of the Earth withers, when the realm of the various animal species dies away, when the present form of the human being is no longer possible, because it is an emanation of the Earth, belonging therefore to the Earth—when everything thus disintegrates as if into nothingness, then the seeds are still there that the Gardener is guiding over into a future formation of the Earthly world, called in my *Occult Science* the Future Jupiter world."

Christ and the Human Soul, Rudolf Steiner, Lecture IV, Norrkoping, July 16, 1914, GA 155

"Spirit also becomes dense, and so our collective Earth-incarnations are united into a spiritual body. This body belongs to us; we need it because we evolve onwards to [Future] Jupiter, and it will be the starting point of our embodiment on [Future] Jupiter. At the end of the Earth [Planetary Condition] we shall stand there with the soul—whatever the particular karma of the soul may be—and we shall stand there before our Earthly relics which have been gathered together by Christ, and we shall have to unite with them in order to pass over with them to [Future] Jupiter.

In the [Future] Jupiter period, Lucifer will send over what has remained of scattered Earth-relics as a dead content of [Future] Jupiter. It will not, as a Moon, separate from [Future] Jupiter; but will be within [Future] Jupiter, and it will be continually thrusting up these Earth-relics. And these Earth-relics will have to be animated as species-souls by the souls above.

And now you will remember what I have told you some years ago: that the human race on [Future] Jupiter will divide itself into those souls who have attained their Earth-goal, who will have attained the goal of [Future] Jupiter, and into those souls who will form a middle kingdom between the human kingdom and the animal kingdom on [Future] Jupiter. These latter will be luciferic souls—luciferic, merely spiritual. They will have their body below, and it will be a direct expression of their whole inner being, but they will be able to direct it only from outside. Two races, the good and the bad, will differentiate themselves from one another on [Future] Jupiter.

A [Future] Venus existence will follow that of [Future] Jupiter, and again there will be an adjustment through the further evolution of the Christ; but it is on [Future] Jupiter that man will realize what it means to be perfected only in his own ego, instead of making the whole Earth his concern. That is something he will have to experience through the whole course of the [Future] Jupiter cycle [Planetary Condition]; for everything he has not permeated with Christ during his Earthly existence may then appear before his spiritual sight."

Theosophy of the Rosicrucians, Rudolf Steiner, Lecture VII,
The Technique of Karma, Munich, May 31, 1907, GA 99

"In the future, the Earth will incarnate as a new planetary body, known as
[Future] Jupiter. The human astral body then will have developed to a stage
where it no longer confronts the physical body as an enemy, as is the case
today, but it will still not have reached its highest stage. The etheric body on
[Future] Jupiter will have reached the stage at which the physical body is now;
for it will then have three planetary evolutions behind it as the physical body
has today.

On the planetary body following [Future] Jupiter, the astral body will
have developed as far as the physical body of today; it will have behind it the
Planetary Condition of [Old] Moon, Earth and [Future] Jupiter evolutions
and will have reached the [Future] Venus evolution. The final planetary
incarnation will be that of [Future] Vulcan, when the "I", the Ego, will have
attained the highest stage of its development. The future incarnations of the
Earth will thus be: [Future] Jupiter, [Future] Venus, and [Future] Vulcan.
These designations are also found in the names of the days of the week."

The Influence of Spiritual Beings Upon Man, Rudolf Steiner,
Lecture VIII, Berlin, May 16, 1908, GA 102

"Beings that stay behind at such stages appear in a later Epoch with
approximately the character of the earlier Age. They have grown together
with it, but not in the forms of the later Epoch. They appear in a later Epoch
as subordinate nature-spirits. In fact, the human race will furnish a whole
number of such new nature-spirits in the second half of the [Future] Jupiter
evolution; for man will have fully completed the Fifth Principle [Spirit-Self,
Manas] at the [Future] Jupiter stage [Planetary Condition]. For those who
have not used the opportunity on Earth to develop the Fifth Principle there
will be no available form. They will appear as nature-spirits, and they will
appear then with Four Principles, the Fourth being the highest. Whereas
the normally advanced man will have the Principles 5, 4, 3, 2 at the [Future]
Jupiter stage [Planetary Condition]; on the other hand, these men will have 4,
3, 2, 1. That would be the destiny of those who have not gradually developed
their Higher Principles by making use of Earthly life. They become nature-

spirits, so to speak, of future evolutionary periods, working invisibly. Just the same occurred in the case of our present nature-spirits in the earlier periods of evolution, except in so far as there are, of course, continual changes according to the character of the different periods. Everything has now been graded, so to speak, according to moral responsibility, and because this is so, the nature-spirits that arise from the human race will have a certain morality. Upon [Future] Jupiter there will be nature-spirits which have moral responsibility.

Let us now recollect what I have said as to how [Future] Jupiter differs from our Earth. We have described the nature of the Earth as that of the planet of Love, in contrast to the nature of the Old Moon, the planet of Wisdom. As love has evolved on Earth so did the wisdom that we find all around us evolve on the Old Moon. Love in its lowest form originated in the ancient Lemurian Age [Third Epoch] and becomes transformed to ever higher stages up to the highest spiritual form. When in the future the Earth planet appears as [Future] Jupiter, the [Future] Jupiter dwellers will direct their gaze upon Love as men on Earth do upon Wisdom. We observe the thigh bone into which wisdom is woven; the whole Earth is in a certain sense crystallized wisdom, which was formed little by little on the [Old] Moon. But wisdom was formed gradually just as on our Earth love is gradually formed. And just as we wonder at the wisdom in all that surrounds us, so he who will one day inhabit [Future] Jupiter will feel wafting towards him the love that will lie in all things. This love will stream forth from all beings and speak to us, as the wisdom speaks to us which is secreted into the Earth through the [Old] Moon existence.

Thus, the Cosmos moves forward from stage to stage. The Earth is the Cosmos of Love, and every condition has its special task. As a common wisdom prevails throughout our Earth, so will a common love prevail throughout [Future] Jupiter.

And as the destructive forces of wisdom originate from those beings who stayed behind on the [Old] Moon, so there will appear upon [Future] Jupiter the destructive forces of love from beings who have remained behind. Into the midst of the general tapestry of the [Future] Jupiter existence will be set the hideous forms of the retarded beings with egoistic demands for love and they will be the mighty devastating powers in the [Future] Jupiter existence.

The staying behind of human beings in individual incarnations creates the destructive nature-powers on [Future] Jupiter. Thus, we see how the world is woven with harmful elements as well as beneficent; we have a moral element woven into the world process."

The Evolution of Consciousness, Rudolf Steiner, Lecture XII, Penmaenmawr, August 30, 1923, GA 227

"In the Future Jupiter Age [Planetary Condition] man will have power to shape himself by his thoughts; in the [Future] Venus-existence [Planetary Condition] he will give form to the world around him. So it is that the thoughts of men point towards the [Future] Jupiter stage in the evolution [Planetary Condition] of the world and of man—a stage that can be reached only when the Earth [Planetary Condition] has passed through death and risen to a new planetary existence. For thoughts will not then live in us in their present fluctuating way; they will take definite shape and appear in the very form of man.

Today we are able to keep our thoughts to ourselves, and on certain occasions our countenance can appear perfectly innocent, although we are inwardly guilty. We shall not be able to do this during the [Future] Jupiter-existence. A man's thoughts will then engender the expression of his face. The human form will have lost its mineralized firmness; it will be inwardly flexible and will consist of a quite soft substance. A wrong thought rising up in us will instantly show itself to other people through a change in our expression. Everything in the nature of a thought will at once take shape; a man will then go about in the guise of his own enduring thoughts and temperament. Hence if, during the [Future] Jupiter-existence, a man is a regular scoundrel, or has only animal impulses, that is what he will look like. That is the first stage in man's future.

The second stage [the Future Venus 6th Planetary Condition] will exemplify the creative power of speech. Today speech arises inwardly and is sent out only into the air. In the future, the spoken word will not fade away into the air but will continue to exist, and with it a man will create actual forms. So that in the [Future] Jupiter age [Planetary Condition] he will have power to shape himself by his thoughts; in the [Future] Venus-existence

[Planetary Condition] he will give form to the world around him. If during the [Future] Venus-existence [Planetary Condition]—when all substance will be as fine as air—he utters an evil word, something like a repulsive plant-form will come into being. Hence a man will be surrounded by the creations of his own speech. During the [Future] Venus- existence [Planetary Condition] creative feelings will arise, creative speech, and the feelings that create through the Word.

During the last metamorphosis of the Earth, the [Future] Vulcan-existence [Planetary Condition], the activities expressed in our walking and the movements of our arms will develop further. During the [Future] Vulcan-existence [Planetary Condition], everything will remain. A man will not simply go about and perform actions; everything he does will leave its imprint on the [Future] Vulcan-existence [Planetary Condition]. His deeds will be actualized, will become realities."

Cosmic and Human Metamorphoses, The Human Soul and the Universe, Rudolf Steiner, Lecture III, February 20, 1917, Berlin, GA 175

"Now we know moreover that man is to undergo further development. The Earth [Planetary Condition] as such will someday come to an end. It will then evolve further, through a [Future] Jupiter, [Future] Venus, and a [Future] Vulcan planetary evolution. Man during this time will rise stage by stage; to his Ego will be added a higher being—the Spirit-Self which will manifest within him. This will reach full manifestation during the [Future] Jupiter evolution [Planetary Condition], which will follow that of our Earth [Planetary Condition]. The Life-Spirit will attain full manifestation in man during the [Future] Venus period [Planetary Condition]; and the actual Spirit-Man during the [Future] Vulcan period [Planetary Condition]. When, therefore, we look forward to the great cosmic future of man, to these three stages of evolution, we look forward to the Spirit-Self, Life-Spirit, and Spirit-Man. But these three which in a sense await us in our future evolution are even now in a certain respect related to us, although they are as yet not in the least developed; for they are still enclosed in the bosom of the divine Spiritual Beings whom we have learnt to know as the Higher Spiritual Hierarchies.

So that today, instead of using the more complicated expression and saying: 'We are in connection with the Hierarchy of the Angels'; we can simply say: 'We are in connection with that which is to come to us in the future—our Spirit-Self.' And instead of saying that we are in connection with the Archangels, we can say: 'We are in connection with what is to come to us in the future, as our Life-Spirit,' and so on."

Esoteric Lessons I, Rudolf Steiner, Number 9, Berlin, May 6, 1906, GA 266

"A man has an organ in himself that fills with air when he inhales and loses this air when he exhales. It fills up with outside air right into its finest branches on inhalation. But spirit lives in the air around us. When a man inhales, he breathes spirit in, and when he exhales, he puts some of the spirit that lives in him into the exhaled air. The spirit develops in him ever more and also outside in the world through the rhythmicized, spirit-filled breath. The spiritual man's growth is promoted through breathing in and out. The most important thing is the spirit that a man puts into his exhaled breath. The spirit is built up by thoughts. A man builds up and streams out his spirit through every thought that he gives along with the exhalation. Man didn't always have an organ to inhale air. Beings breathed fire instead of air on [Old] Moon [Planetary Condition]. Just as we breathe oxygen in and out, so they breathed fire in and cold out. Future men will no longer breathe air. Just as a man prepares his warmth by feeding his warmth organ, the heart, with the blood circulation, through air streaming in from outside, so he will later have an inner air organ through which his organism will be supplied with what we now take in from the atmosphere. A man prepares his own warmth, that on [Old] Moon had been directly sucked in from the environment by the beings there. A man will be able to elaborate the used-up air in his interior. Later on, he will no longer live in an outer air. On [Future] Jupiter [Planetary Condition] he'll live in light and inhale light just as we inhale air now and inhaled warmth on old Moon.

> Overcoming of physical love or development of astral body and transformation into Spirit-Self, ennoblement of animal kingdom... Wisdom

Rhythmization of breathing or development of the etheric body and transformation into Life-Spirit, elevation of the plant kingdom... Beauty

Radiation of kundalini or development of physical body, transformation into Spirit-Man, elevation of mineral kingdom... Power [Strength]

When all of this has happened, the mineral kingdom will pass over into a kind of plant kingdom, then the latter into an animal kingdom, etc. until the next Round [Planetary Condition]."

The Apocalypse of St. John, Rudolf Steiner, Lecture VII, June 24, 1908, GA 104

"Only in the course of the [Old] Moon evolution [Planetary Condition] was wisdom poured into the various beings and creations, so that it was there by the time the Earth [Planetary Condition] came forth from the twilight. All things are now filled with wisdom. And as man today looks into his environment and sees wisdom in everything, so will he, when he has reached [the Future] Jupiter [Planetary Condition], see all the beings around him in a remarkable way. They will pour out something like the fragrance of blissful love. Love will stream forth from all things, and it is the mission of the Earth-evolution [Planetary Condition] to develop this love. Love will then flow through everything, just as wisdom is now in everything. And this love is poured into earthly evolution by man's gradually learning to develop love.

Between the Atlantean Epoch [4th] and that which will come after the War of All against All we have our Epoch [5th], which we have described. In a certain way that which existed previously, that which was in the Atlantean Epoch, will be repeated after our Epoch; but there will be a very great difference. In the Atlantean Epoch man had a dreamy, hazy, clairvoyant consciousness, and when he ascended into the higher worlds his clear self-consciousness faded and he then felt himself within the group-soul. After the great War of All against All man will again see into the higher worlds in a certain way. He will again have the former hazy clairvoyance; but in addition, he will possess what he has gradually acquired in the external physical world.

.Between the Atlantean Flood and the great War of All against All man has had to renounce for a time the power to see into the spiritual world. He has had to content himself with seeing only what is around him in the physical world, in the so-called waking consciousness. This is now the normal condition. But in its place, it has become possible for him fully to develop his self-consciousness, his individual "I," during this time, to feel himself within his skin as a separate "I"-personality, so to speak. This he has won. Now he also retains this individuality when he again rises into the higher spiritual worlds, and this ascent will be possible to him after the great War of All against All. But this ascent would not have been possible if he had not taken part in that great cosmic event in the middle of our Epoch which runs its course in the physical world, as was shown in the last lecture. Man would have been obliged to sink down into a kind of Abyss had he not been preserved from it by the entry of Christ into our world. We must keep in mind that man has descended completely into the physical world in this epoch of ours.

He would remain united with the body and go down into the Abyss. And because of not having used the power of the spirit, the external shape would again come to resemble the previous form. The man who descends into the Abyss would become animal-like. Thus, humanity will realize what we have already indicated. Those who use the life in the body merely as an opportunity to gain the "I"-consciousness will descend into the Abyss and form the evil race. They have turned away from the impulse of Christ Jesus; and from the ugliness of their souls they will again create the animal form man possessed in former times. The evil race, with their savage impulses, will dwell in animal form in the Abyss. And when up above those who have spiritualized themselves, who have received the Christ-Principle, announce what they have to say regarding their union with the name, Christ Jesus—here below in the Abyss will sound forth names of blasphemy and of hatred of that which brings about the spiritual transformation.

It will be somewhat different in the next Epoch which will succeed all these. There will not be a colony limited to one place; but from the general body of humanity will everywhere be recruited those who are mature enough to form the good, the noble, the beautiful side of the next civilization, after the War of All against All. This again is a progress as compared with the earlier Atlantean Epoch when the colony developed in one small place; but with us there is the possibility that from all races of the world will be recruited those who really understand the call of the Earth mission, who raise up Christ within themselves, who develop the principle of brotherly love over the whole Earth; and indeed, in the true sense, not in the sense of the Christian confessions, but in the sense of the true esoteric Christianity which can proceed from every civilization. Those who understand this Christ-Principle will be there in the period [Epoch] following the great War of All against All. After our present purely intellectual civilization, which is now developing in the direction of the Abyss of intellect—and you will find that this is the case in every field of life—there will come a time when man will be the slave of the intelligence, the slave of the personality in which he will sink. Today there is only one way of preserving the personality, and that is to spiritualize it. Those who develop the spiritual life will belong to the small band of the "sealed" from all nations and races, who will appear in white garments after the War of All against All.

Before the Sixth Age of Civilization [6th Post-Atlantean Period], represented by the Community of Philadelphia, we shall experience something like a mighty marriage of peoples, a marriage between intelligence and intellect and spirituality.

This is only mentioned as a symptom of the future Age when the spirituality of the East will unite with the intellectuality of the West. From this union will proceed the Age of Philadelphia [6th Post-Atlantean Period]. All those will participate in this marriage who take into themselves the impulse of Christ Jesus and they will form the great brotherhood which will survive the Great War [of All against All], which will experience enmity and persecution, but will provide the foundation for the good race. After this Great War [of All against All] has brought out the animal nature in those who have remained in the old forms, the good race will arise, and this race will carry over into the future that which is to be the spiritually elevated culture of that future Epoch [6th Epoch]. We shall also have the experience that in our Epoch [5th Epoch], between the great Atlantean Flood and the great War of All against All, in the Age represented by the community at Philadelphia [6th Post-Atlantean Period], a colony is being formed, the members of which will not emigrate but will be everywhere; so that everywhere there will be some who are working in the sense of the community of Philadelphia, in the sense of the binding together of humanity, in the sense of the Christ-Principle."

The Apocalypse of St. John, Rudolf Steiner, Lecture IX, June 26, 1908, GA 104

"In our description of the evolution of man we have now reached the point when, after the Epoch characterized by the sounding of the seven trumpets, the Earth with all its beings passes into another condition, when the physical dissolves, so to speak, and changes into spiritual, but first into astral. An astral Earth arises and into it passes all the beings who are ripe for it, that is, who have become capable of overcoming even their material part and using it in the service of the spiritual. On the other hand, those who are unable to spiritualize the bodily, material part, who cling to the material, are thrown out and form a sort of secondary Earth [a moon-planetoid, as it were], the study of which is very instructive for gaining knowledge of the future destiny of humanity. But to this end it is necessary that we clearly understand what has become, during this astralizing of our Earth, of those who have reached the necessary degree of maturity, who have taken the Christ-Principle into themselves and allowed it to become active.

The greater portion of humanity will only have gained the power to work quite consciously in the Spirit-Self, in the transformed astral body, at the close of the Earth evolution.

All men now possess the rudiments of the Spirit-Self, but one has more, another less. Many will still have to go through many incarnations before they have developed the Spirit-Self far enough to become aware of what they are working upon within their human nature. But when the Earth has reached its goal, when the seventh trumpet begins to sound, the following will be observed: that which exists of the physical body will be dissolved like salt in warm water. The human Spirit-Self will be developed to a high degree, so that man will repeat again and again the words of Paul, "Not I, but Christ in me does everything." This will enable him to dissolve the physical nature and make the ennobled etheric into a being which can live in the astralized Earth. Thus man, a new being, will live over into this spiritualized Earth.

The earthly bodies will be dissolved, the celestial will appear as the luminous expression of what the soul is. 'It is sown corruptible and will rise incorruptible.' The incorruptible body will then be resurrected. Paul calls the etheric or life-body, spiritual body, after the physical has dissolved and the etheric passes into the astral Earth.

Today man works upon his soul; in this way he makes his body more and more like the soul, and when the Earth has arrived at the end of its mission his body will have become an outward image of the soul which has taken Christ into itself. Such a man will survive and implant in the next embodiment of our Earth the forces he has thus developed. [The Future] Jupiter will have an appearance such as men are able to bring about by constructing it out of their own bodies. This [Future] Jupiter will, to begin with, receive its form from that which man has made for himself. Imagine that all the bodies you have fashioned are united in a single cosmic Globe; that will be [Future] Jupiter. In your soul you have the germs of the future form of Jupiter, and of the forces it will contain. And out of [the Future] Jupiter will be born the Jupiter beings. Thus, man is now preparing for the birth of the Jupiter bodies.

What, therefore, must man do in order to give a worthy form to the future embodiment of our Earth? He must take care that the work he can now do consciously is done in the Christian way, so that the etheric body (which will be an image of this work) will enter worthily into the spiritualized Earth. All the parts of this body will be just as man has made them. He will bring into this spiritual Earth what he has made of his physical body, and this will be the foundation for his future evolution. Just as your present soul develops in your present body, which you have inherited from the [Old] Moon [Planetary Condition], the future soul will develop in that which you yourselves make out of your own body. Hence the body is described as that which envelops the soul, which clothes the "I," which is inhabited by the "I," as the temple of the selfhood within, the temple of the Divinity dwelling in man, the Temple of God. When, therefore, you form this body you are building a future temple, that is to say, the new incarnation of the Earth. You build up [the Future] Jupiter [Planetary Condition] in the right way by shaping the human body in the right way." What, therefore, must appear when the Earth has reached its goal? A temple of the soul harmonious in all its measurements. Hence the

Initiate is commissioned to examine this temple which man will then have built. When this temple of God is measured it will be made manifest whether the soul has done what is right. That is the temple in which are to live the new beings in the [Future] Jupiter period... [Planetary Condition]"

The Apocalypse of St. John, Rudolf Steiner, Lecture X, June 27, 1908, GA 104

"During the [Future] Jupiter period [Planetary Condition], man will rise to a still higher degree of consciousness of which most people today have no inkling. Then, when man is saved, so to speak, when he has risen from the Abyss or escaped from decadence, when he has risen into the astralized and spiritual Earth, this will be the foundation for his attainment upon [Future] Jupiter of the consciousness which we may call the "conscious picture-consciousness." If this is to be described, it can only be done from the experiences of the Initiates. For initiation is indeed nothing but the acquisition of the capacity to attain at an earlier stage of evolution what normal humanity will gain at a later stage. In the conscious picture-consciousness man is just as self-conscious as he is today from morning to evening – but he perceives not only the external objects, but [also] in his soul's field of vision he has pictures. Indeed, they are pictures which are by no means dim, but rather are incorporated in the clear consciousness of day. Thus, the clear day-consciousness [Earth] plus the [Old] Moon-consciousness gives the [Future] Jupiter-consciousness. Man keeps what he now has and in addition gains the capacity of perceiving the elements of soul and spirit.

Now suppose a person hardened himself during our Epoch against the Christ-Principle and were to come to the time of the great War of All against All without having had the Christ-experience, suppose he were to come to this time and had thrust the Christ away from him, then when the Earth passes over into the astral [at the end of Earth evolution], that which was there and which he ought to have changed, would spring forth, it would spring forth in its old form. The beast with the seven heads and ten horns would appear; whereas in those who have received the Christ-Principle, sex will again be overcome. The hardened ones will keep the six-horned sexuality and will appear in their totality as the beast with the seven heads and ten horns of which the rudiments were laid down in the Atlantean Epoch. They will be transformed through the reception of the Christ-Impulse; but if Christ is rejected they will remain and will reappear in the Epoch indicated by the falling of the vials of wrath and the Earth splitting, as it were, into two parts, one in which the Christ-men appear with white garments as the Elect, even in the Epoch of the seals; and the other part in which men appear in the form of the beast with seven heads and ten horns."

Reading the Pictures of the Apocalypse, Rudolf Steiner, Lecture X, May 19, 1909, GA 104a

"We have seen how the writer of the Apocalypse indicates that in the Fifth Age [Epoch], after the War of All against All, people will appear in white garments, that the Sixth Age [Epoch] is characterized by the Earth's enduring great tremors and earthquakes as the result of materialism, and that the spiritual human beings will be the sealed ones.

We must point out that just as the angels or angeloi underwent their human stage in earlier planetary incarnations, humanity must also ascend through its development. What confronts us today as nature is the achievement of the gods. In the future, human beings will also accomplish divine spiritual deeds. We are speaking of the time when the human being will already have begun to work with magic from the periphery of the Earth, out of the realm of the invisible. However, in contrast to the sealed human beings there will also be those who have chained themselves to matter. These materialistic people will have been pushed down. This is why the writer of the Apocalypse sees the spiritualized people hovering above with the others bound to matter below. He sees this very clearly the moment the seventh seal is broken to reveal a vision of the future.

Then comes the next [Epoch] of seven Ages [Periods]. Here the writer of the Apocalypse sees Devachan [Heaven] and hears it prophetically proclaimed in the blowing of trumpets. Human beings will look down upon the Earth itself as it becomes increasingly material; only the coarsest humankind will have consciously reacquired clairvoyance. In the Age of the Trumpets the Lemurian Age [3rd Epoch] will resurrect; human beings will be close to God for they will have completely spiritualized themselves. In the Lemurian Age the Earth still existed entirely within the element of fire. Human beings lived in fire before descending into a dense bodily nature—this will be repeated in a spiritual state. When the seventh trumpet sounds forth a kind of blessed state will come upon humanity. Then we come to a repetition of the time when the Sun was separated from the Earth. The human being, together with the Earth, will have advanced to the time when the Sun again unites with the Earth. The Earth will pass over into what is called an astral state. Human beings able to live in the astral world will raise up the finer part of the Earth and then be united with the Sun. The portion of the Earth that has remained coarse will be united with the Moon to form a new kind of Moon. The kind of conditions prevailing during the Hyperborean Age [2nd Epoch] will enter in again, but at a higher stage of evolution. This is characterized by the "Woman clothed with the Sun" and having the Moon at her feet. The beasts that rise up out of the sea or fall from heaven also belong to this whole stream of evolution that is pictured, as if captured in a moment of time. (Revelation 12:1–13:10)."

Reading the Pictures of the Apocalypse, Rudolf Steiner, Lecture XI, May 20, 1909, GA 104a

"All the beings who cannot rise up into the higher world must go down into this lower world. All the higher beings, after the Age of the Seven Trumpet calls, will enter into a state of the Earth united again with the Sun.

When the Sun will have again united with the Earth, then human beings—through the fact that they will have purified their instincts, desires, and passions—will redeem the luciferic beings. The luciferic beings who do not go on to the Sun remain in their original condition. They then appear as expelled into the evil, lower astral world. This is the ancient snake, and it emerges as the first dragon. Therefore, when the Earth enters the Sun, a dragon appears. But there are yet other beings left behind: such human beings who could not prevent themselves from dropping back into animality, who remain slaves to their animal instincts. While the other human beings go to the Sun, these will form an evil power over and against the higher. These form the second monster, and the writer of the Apocalypse says in his exact fashion: The luciferic dragon appears in heaven because he comes from higher worlds; the second beast arises from the sea—this consists of the souls of animalistic human beings who have remained behind. (Compare: Rev. 12:3-13:10)

We have still a third vision, that of the black magicians. They do not remain stuck in animality; they develop spiritual abilities. In full consciousness they have turned away and provide a bodily incarnation for Sorath. That will be the incarnation in flesh of the Demon of the Sun.

But then we see how the Earth emerges from the Sun yet again in the future. If the spiritual human beings were to remain united with the Sun forever, then the other human beings who, without guilt, had remained behind in animality would never be saved. So, these spiritualized people come forth once more and unite with what has fallen out of evolution in an attempt to save these backward souls. When the Earth began its existence as "Earth" it had to briefly repeat the [Old] Saturn, [Old] Sun, and [Old] Moon [Planetary] Conditions once again. It went through recapitulations of those Conditions before it became the present-day Earth. Now, when actual Earth Conditions prevail, it must prophetically mirror the future embodiments of [Future] Jupiter, [Future] Venus, and [Future] Vulcan. In this way the Earth [Planetary Condition] goes through seven states during its actual Earth Condition. These states are usually called "Rounds." During the prophetically mirrored Jupiter state [Planetary Condition], the Earth will actually unite with the Sun. On this [Future] Jupiter-Earth [Planetary Condition] all the great Cultural Ages will appear again—with the seven intervals between them - but they will be far less sharply delineated. On this [Future] Jupiter-Earth, many beings still have the possibility of being saved, even the black magicians.

This will also be the case on [the Future] Venus-Earth [Planetary Condition], when we have a Sixth planetary interval. Here also the beings that have remained behind will stubbornly struggle against help; but this [Future] Venus-Earth will at last be decisive.

Then, on the [Future] Vulcan-Earth, nothing more can be saved. On [Future] Venus- Earth, the last moment for salvation will come in the last Sub-Epoch. That is why the ancient cabalists formed the word "Sorath," because the number 666 is contained within it. That is also the number of those human beings who, out of their own cunning free will, have become black magicians by placing spiritual forces in the service of their own egotism.

The first dragon is not a human being. It came out of the spiritual world. The second dragon is ascribed to animalistic nature; but in a fundamental sense, the Bible ascribes this number of the third group to human beings. So, the number 666 is not a sign of the beast but a human number.

The Apocalypse is an outline of the whole of evolution. [Future] Venus-Earth is portrayed to clairvoyant sight in such a way that there is not much hope for those left behind. Human powers at that time will not be capable of very much. That is why everything appears so desolate, and the worst vices will reign there in the most depraved ways. They must be expelled during the [Future] Venus state of the Earth. On the [Future] Jupiter-Earth there are still many, many who will allow themselves to be saved and who will unite with the Sun.

But during the [Future] Venus-Earth, evil must be overcome and driven into the Abyss; that is the "Fall of Babylon." (Revelation 17–18) The people who have been saved can develop themselves further to a new Sun state. What has been cleansed and purified will arise for the [Future] Vulcan-Earth.

The place that humanity has prepared and will find waiting is called the "New Jerusalem" by the writer of the Apocalypse. A new world will arise, inhabitable by human beings who will have achieved the requisite state of maturity. In a new state, in the [Future] Jupiter existence, they will find the place where, out of love and out of human work, peace will reign."

Reading the Pictures of the Apocalypse, Rudolf Steiner, Lecture XII, May 21, 1909, GA 104a

"In the age of "Philadelphia" the "I" will permeate the Spirit-Self, or Manas. Then the human beings who, through theosophical-spiritual teachings, have made themselves capable of recognizing Christ will be in a position to see him in a new form of existence - in his delicate etheric body—for he will come again.

The I will be educated through wisdom, through Theosophy, so that it receives Manas or Spirit-Self and will be able to recognize Christ again. Theosophical teachings have been given to humankind not in order to agitate for Theosophy but rather because they were necessary.

In the Age [Epoch] represented by the Seven Seals something like a shower of meteorites will occur, caused by increasing materialism, and some human beings will ascend to a spiritual state. What the spiritualized human beings have acquired through their efforts in our Post-Atlantean Age [Epoch] will completely permeate them within. When, in the Age of the Sixth Seal, everything that the human being has in terms of sentient soul, intellectual soul, and consciousness soul has been worked into the other members, human beings will have achieved the ability to create an external imprint of their inner life in their gesture, features, in their whole life. Because they have worked on their development, they will be able in the Fourth, Fifth, and Sixth Ages [Cultural Periods, Sub-Epochs] in the Epoch of the Seals, to use these three soul forces—the sentient, intellectual, and consciousness souls—to permeate and work on themselves in order to take in Manas [Spirit-Self].

"Then the various groups of people who have matured will be united in the community of Philadelphia [6th Cultural Period, Sub-Epoch] for mature brotherhood when every soul will feel for others. All those who have been separated out of the various groups can now be multiplied together because they will live within one another. Their life together will be such that they will not disturb one another, such that one soul will work into another soul in complete harmony. Twelve times 12,000 gives the number 144,000.

These are the people who will constitute human society in the Age of the Sixth Seal [6th Epoch] ... In the Age when the sixth seal is broken the "people of twelve" will appear. The salvation of the "great whore of Babylon" will also occur in the Sixth Age [6th Epoch]. In this Sixth Age the Earth will have repeated the [Old] Saturn, [Old] Sun, and [Old] Moon stages, as well as the Earth Sixth Age [Planetary] Condition itself and [the Future] Jupiter-Earth. On [the Future] Venus-Earth the Earth will finally have the five Rounds [Planetary Conditions] behind it. Then the Sixth State will have come. [6th Planetary Condition] Nevertheless, the [Future] Vulcan state [7th Planetary Condition] for the chosen will not be present yet.

But those who have proven themselves to be immature in the Age of [the Future] Venus-Earth, who have placed themselves under the rulership of Sorath, must now isolate themselves on a special sphere of Earth [8th Sphere] while the other seven proceed downward and again upward. Thus, the colony of Sorath falls away. The black magicians inhabit this Eighth Sphere, which goes to the left and away, and the beast gives a home to all that thus falls away: that is the Eighth state [Sphere].

The lamb, who will be the lord over the lower nature, forms one of the seals. Sorat is as if expelled in the Eighth Sphere by the woman who shows us another seal of the Rosicrucian. The seer can also see this in the spiritual world. In this way, these Rosicrucian seals have an awakening effect when we meditate upon them with Understanding."

Reading the Pictures of the Apocalypse, Rudolf Steiner, Lecture XI, May 20, 1909, GA 104a

"But [Old] Saturn, [Old] Sun, and [Old] Moon [Planetary Conditions] occurred before the middle of the Earth's evolution. Those beings who remained behind before the midpoint have made an offering, a sacrifice. However, those who remain behind from now on, after the middle of the Earth's evolution, merely represent a hindrance, not a sacrifice.

But then we see how the Earth emerges from the Sun yet again in the future. If the spiritual human beings were to remain united with the Sun forever, then the other human beings who, without guilt, had remained behind in animality would never be saved. So, these spiritualized people come forth once more and unite with what has fallen out of evolution in an attempt to save these backward souls. When the Earth began its existence as "Earth" it had to briefly repeat the Old Saturn, Old Sun, and Old Moon [Planetary] Conditions once again. It went through recapitulations of those conditions before it became the present-day Earth. Now, when actual Earth conditions prevail, it must prophetically mirror the future embodiments of Future Jupiter, Future Venus, and Future Vulcan [Planetary Conditions]. In this way the Earth goes through seven states during its actual Earth [Planetary] Condition. These states are usually called "Rounds." During the prophetically mirrored Future Jupiter state [Planetary Condition], the Earth will actually unite with the Sun. On this Future Jupiter-Earth [incarnation or Planetary Condition] all the great Cultural Ages will appear again—with the seven intervals between them—but they will be far less sharply delineated. On this Future Jupiter-Earth [incarnation or Planetary Condition], many beings still have the possibility of being saved, even the black magicians.

The Apocalypse is an outline of the whole of evolution. Venus-Earth is portrayed to clairvoyant sight in such a way that there is not much hope for those left behind. Human powers at that time will not be capable of very much. That is why everything appears so desolate and the worst vices will reign there in the most depraved ways. They must be expelled during the Venus state of the earth. On the Future Jupiter-Earth there are still many, many who will allow themselves to be saved and who will unite with the Sun.

The place that humanity has prepared and will find waiting is called the "New Jerusalem" by the writer of the Apocalypse. A new world will arise, inhabitable by human beings who will have achieved the requisite state of maturity. In a new state, in the Future Jupiter existence, they will find the place where, out of love and out of human work, peace will reign."

The Apocalypse of St. John, Rudolf Steiner, Lecture XII, June 30, 1908, GA 104

"Humanity will finally be divided into beings who practice white magic and those who practice black magic. Thus, in the mystery of 666, or Sorath, is hidden the secret of black magic; and the tempter to black magic, that most fearful crime in the Earth evolution, with which no other crimes can be compared, this seducer is represented by the writer of the Apocalypse as the two-horned beast. Thus, there appears on our horizon, so to speak, the division of humanity in the far distant future; the chosen of Christ, who finally will be the white magicians, and the adversaries, the terrible wizards, the black magicians who cannot escape from matter and whom the writer of the Apocalypse describes as those who make prostitution with matter. Hence this whole practice of black magic, the union which takes place between man and the hardening in matter is presented to him in the spiritual vision of the Great Babylon, the community made up of all those who carry on black magic; in the frightful marriage, or rather, unrestrained marriage, between man and the forces of prostituted matter.

And thus, in the far future, we see two powers confronting each other; on the one hand those who swell the population of the Great Babylon, and on the other hand chose who rise above matter, who as human beings unite with the principle represented as the Lamb. We see how on the one hand the blackest ones segregate themselves in Babylon, led by all the forces opposing the Sun, by Sorath the two-horned beast, and we see those who have developed from the Elect, who unite with Christ, or the Lamb, who appears to them; the marriage of the Lamb on the one hand, and that of Babylon, the descending Babylon, on the other! We see Babylon descend into the Abyss, and the Elect, who have celebrated the marriage with the Lamb, rise to the exercise of the forces of white magic. And as they not only recognize the spiritual forces but also understand how to operate then magically, they are able to prepare what they possess in the Earth for the next planetary incarnation, [the Future] Jupiter.

They sketch out the great outlines, so to speak, which [Future] Jupiter is to have. We see the preparatory forms, which are to survive as the forms of the next Earth incarnation, as [the Future] Jupiter, come forth by the power of the white magicians: we see the New Jerusalem produced by white magic. But that which is described as Sorath—666 - must first be expelled. That which has succumbed to the principle of the two- horned beast, and hence has hardened itself into the beast with the seven heads and ten horns, is driven forth. The power by which the Sun-Genius overcomes those who are expelled, which drives them down into the Abyss, is called the countenance of the Sun-Genius and the countenance of the Sun-Genius is Michael, who, as the representative, so to speak, of the Sun-Genius, overcomes the beast with the two horns, the seducer, which is also called the great dragon. This is represented to the seer in the picture of Michael who has the key, who stands by the side of God and holds the opposing forces chained.

From these lectures it may be seen that for those who now turn to a spiritual conception of the world, in order to live beyond the great War into the Sixth Epoch (which is represented by the opening of the seals), there is the possibility to receive the Christ-Principle. They will be able to receive the spiritual elements which are laid down in the Age signified by the community at Philadelphia [6th Cultural Period, Sub-Epoch], and in the near future they will manifest a strong tendency towards becoming spiritual. Those who turn today to a spiritual view receive a powerful disposition to enter upon the upward path.

We know that the Earth will be followed by its next incarnation, [Future] Jupiter. When man has reached [the Future] Jupiter, he will appear as a different being. The Jupiter-man will have thoroughly worked from his "I" upon his astral body; and when today we say, The Earth-man who stands before us in the waking condition has developed: physical body, etheric body, astral body and "I," we must say of the Jupiter-man: he will have developed physical body, etheric body, astral body and "I" but he will have changed his astral body into Spirit-Self. He will live at a higher stage of consciousness, a stage which may be described as follows: The ancient dim-picture-consciousness of the [Old] Moon, which existed also in the first Epochs of the Earth-consciousness, will again be there with its pictures as clairvoyant consciousness; but it will be furnished with the human "I," so that with this Jupiter-consciousness man will reflect as logically as he does now with his day-consciousness on the Earth..

The Jupiter-man therefore will possess spiritual vision of a certain degree. Part of the soul-world will lie open to him; he will perceive the pleasure and pain of those around him in pictures which will arise in his imaginative consciousness. He will therefore live under entirely different moral conditions. Now imagine that as a Jupiter- man you have a human soul before you. The pain and pleasure of this soul will arise in pictures before you. The pictures of the pain of the other soul will distress you, and if you do not remove the other's pain it will be impossible for you to feel happy. The pictures of sorrow and suffering would torment the Jupiter-man with his exalted consciousness if he were to do nothing to alleviate this sorrow and thus at the same time remove his own distressing pictures which are nothing but the expression of the sorrow around him! It will not be possible for one to feel pleasure or pain without others also feeling it.

Only the Initiate can become conscious of these effects today, but men are gradually developing towards this consciousness. Those who reach the goal of the Earth evolution will then have an astral body completely permeated by the "I," and by the spiritual content which it will have formed. They will have this consciousness as a result, as a fruit of the Earth evolution, and will carry it over into the Jupiter evolution. We might say that when the Earth period has thus come to an end, man will have gained capacities which are symbolically represented by the building of the New Jerusalem. Man will then already look into that picture-world of [Future] Jupiter; the Spirit-Self will then be fully developed in him. That is the goal of the Earth evolution.

Upon [the Future] Jupiter [Planetary Condition], when he has transformed his astral body, he will be able to work into this etheric body also, but today he cannot do this; he still needs helpers, so to speak. Upon [Future] Jupiter he will be capable of beginning the real work on the etheric body.

Thus we shall be able to characterize in another way the two kinds of men which we find at the end of the Earth's evolution. We have those who have received the Christ-Principle and thus transformed their astral body, and who have gained the help of Christ to transform the etheric body also. And we have the others who did not come to the Christ-Principle; who also were unable to change anything in the etheric body, for they could not find the helper, Christ.

This second death passes unnoticed over those who have made their etheric body harmonize with the astral body through the reception of the Christ-Principle. The second death has no power over them. But the others feel the second death when they have to pass over into the future astral form. The condition of humanity will then be such that those who have reached the goal of evolution will have entirely permeated their astral body with Christ. They will be ready to pass over to [Future] Jupiter. Upon our Earth they have made the plan of the [Future] Jupiter evolution. This is the plan which is called the New Jerusalem. They live in a New Heaven and a New Earth, that is, [the Future] Jupiter. This new Jupiter will be accompanied by a satellite, composed of those who are excluded from the life in the spiritual, who have experienced the second death and are, therefore, unable to attain the [Future] Jupiter consciousness.

Thus we have such men as have pressed forward to the [Future] Jupiter consciousness, who have attained to Spirit-Self; and such beings as have thrust away the forces which would have given them this consciousness. They are those who only upon [Future] Jupiter have attained to the "I"-consciousness of the Earth, who exist there, so to speak, as man now exists on the Earth with his four members. But such a man can develop himself only on the Earth, the Earth alone has the environment, the ground, the air, the clouds, the plants, the minerals which are necessary to man if he wishes to gain what may be gained within the four members. [Future] Jupiter will be quite differently formed, it will be a new Earth, soil, air, water, everything will be different. It will be impossible for beings who have only gained the Earth consciousness to live a normal life; they will be backward beings.

But now comes something more for our comfort. Even on [Future] Jupiter, there is still a last possibility, through the strong powers which the advanced will have, to move those fallen beings to turn back and even to convert a number. Only with the [Future] Venus incarnation of the Earth will come the last decision, the unalterable decision. When we reflect upon all this, the thought we recently considered will be seen in a new light. It will no longer call forth anxiety and disquietude, but only the determination: 'I will do everything necessary to fulfill the earth mission.'"

The Apocalypse of St. John, Rudolf Steiner, Lecture X, June 27, 1908, GA 104

"If you clearly understand that in the course of our evolution we have seven Conditions of Consciousness, you will also perceive how this is connected with what is described in our various books. They are cosmic systems. You will there read that our Earth developed out of an ancient planetary system which is described as [Old] Moon. We then went further back from the [Old] Moon to the [Old] Sun, and from the [Old] Sun to [Old] Saturn. Each of these conditions is divided into the seven Conditions of Life—formerly called Rounds; Rounds are the same as Conditions of Life. And those now called Conditions of Form were formerly called Globes; Rounds are the same as conditions of life. And those now called conditions of form were formerly called globes. The latter expression was extremely misleading, for it led to the idea that these seven globes were side by side.

These conditions, from the most remote form, which was almost formless, down through the physical and up again to the formless, are not seven Globes existing side by side, but seven successive conditions. The same Globe that is now physical was first of all spiritual, then it became denser and denser. It is the same Globe simply condensed. Then a portion of it became astral, then a portion physical; it is always the same Globe. It dissolves again like salt in warm water, it again becomes astral. We have ascended to this astral where, in the Apocalypse, the vials of wrath are described; there the Earth becomes astral again.

We have seen that we pass through 343 Conditions of Form [7x7x7 = 343]. Now, the subject grows more complicated when we learn that the matter does not end here, but that man must also pass through various Conditions with each Condition of Form. In our mineral condition of life during the Earth period three Conditions of Form have preceded the present physical Condition of Form and three others will follow it. But now the physical again passes through seven Conditions, and these are the seven of which we have spoken in previous lectures; the First when the Sun is still united with the Earth, the Second when it separates, the Third when the moon withdraws, the Fourth that of the Atlantean humanity. The Atlantean humanity lives in the Fourth Epoch of the development of the physical Condition of Form. Thus, within each Condition of Form you have again seven Epochs or so-called root-races, although the expression "race" applies only to the middle Condition. We are now living in the Fifth Epoch, the 5th Post-Atlantean Epoch, between the great Atlantean Flood and the great War of All against All. The Sixth Epoch will follow this and then the Seventh Epoch. The Sixth Epoch is indicated in the Apocalypse of John by the seven seals, and the Seventh [Epoch] by the seven trumpets. Then the Earth passes over into the astral. That is a new Condition of Form which again will have its seven Epochs.

And still our diagram is not at an end. Each Epoch as it runs its course between such events as the great Atlantean Flood and the great War of All against All must again be divided into seven Ages [Periods]. As regards the Fifth Epoch there are the Indian Age of Civilization [1st Post-Atlantean Period], the Persian Age of Civilization [2nd Post-Atlantean Period], the Assyrian-Babylonian-Chaldean- Egyptian-Jewish Age of Civilization [3rd Post-Atlantean Period], the Graeco-Latin Age [of Civilization, 4th Post-Atlantean Period], our own Age [of Civilization 5th Post-Atlantean Period], then the Sixth [Age of Civilization, 6th Post-Atlantean Period], which is indicated in the Apocalypse by the community of Philadelphia, and the Seventh Age of Civilization [7th Post-Atlantean Period] which will follow that.

Thus if we imagine the whole of evolution consisting of nothing but short ages such as these—which, however, are long enough—we have $7 \times 7 \times 7 \times 7 \times 7$ stages of development such as the ancient Indian or the ancient Persian. The number of different conditions of this nature which man passes through between Saturn and Vulcan is 16807:

$$7 \times 7 \times 7 = 343.$$
$$7 \times 343 = 2401.$$
$$7 \times 2401 = 16807.$$

Thus you see how the number 7 governs development in the successive periods throughout the whole of evolution. Just as the tones in music progress from octave to octave, so does the whole of evolution take place in octaves of development."

From Zodiac to Solar System

The Influence of Spiritual Beings on the Human Being, Rudolf Steiner, Lecture II, January 27, 1908, GA 102

"What has been achieved in a planetary existence and has become Sun ascends to "heavenly" existence and becomes Zodiacal existence. And having reached Zodiacal existence, what does it do? It offers itself in sacrifice! Please take account of this particular word. The first dawn-condition of the Earth, [Old] Saturn, arose in a mysterious way as the result of sacrifice on the part of the Zodiac. The forces which caused the first, rarefied [Old] Saturn-masses to gather together were those which streamed down from the Zodiac, producing on [Old] Saturn the first germinal inception of physical man. This continued without cessation. You must not picture it as happening only once. Fundamentally speaking, what is happening continuously is that within what we call a Planetary System the forces which evolved to a higher stage after having themselves passed through a Planetary System, are sacrificed. We can say in effect: what is at first contained in a Planetary System evolves to a "Sun" existence, then to "Zodiacal" existence and then has the power to be itself creative, to offer itself in sacrifice within a planetary existence.

The forces from the Zodiac "rain" down continuously into the planetary existence and continuously ascend again; for that which at one time became our Zodiac must gradually ascend again. The distribution of forces in our Earth existence may be conceived as follows: on the one side forces are descending from the Zodiac and, on the other, forces are ascending to the Zodiac. Such is the mysterious interplay between the Zodiac and our Earth.

Forces descend and forces ascend. This is the mysterious "heavenly ladder" upon which forces are descending and ascending.

As far as our human understanding goes, these forces began to descend during the [Old] Saturn-existence of our Earth and when the Earth-existence proper had reached its middle point, the stage had arrived when they gradually began again to ascend. We have now passed beyond the middle point of our evolution, which fell in the middle of the Atlantean Epoch; and what human beings have lived through since then is a phase of existence beyond the middle point. In a certain sense, therefore, we may say that at the present time, more forces are ascending to the Zodiac than are descending from it.

In this way you will realize that there is interaction between everything in Cosmic Space, that everything in Cosmic Space is interconnected, inter-related. But it must never be forgotten that these operations and activities are going on all the time, that they are ever-present. At any given moment in our evolution, we can therefore speak of forces which are going forth from man and forces which are coming in; forces are descending, and forces are ascending. For all and each of these forces there comes, at some point, the moment when from being descending forces they are transformed into ascending forces. All forces which eventually become ascending forces are at first descending forces. They descend, so to say, as far as man. In man they acquire the power to ascend."

Conclusion

There can be no proper conclusion to our presentation on *How to Become an Angel* because it is an unfolding process that is never-ending. You can see by the many descriptions of the process of Angel-hood that each person is responsible for advancing towards their higher spirit in super-nature, or moving backwards into sub-nature and the Eighth Sphere. These are the choices and consequences of having been bestowed with freedom. Each person is responsible for their own karma, good or bad. Even the pace of progressive spiritual evolution is determined by the individual. It should also be obvious, by now, that a host of spiritual beings are anxious to help with each human's embodiment of their Angelic nature.

Progressing up the ranks of the spiritual hierarchy happens with each new Globe, Round, Epoch, and Period. The constant growth of each rank of the spiritual hierarchy creates never-ending change and interaction with a family of beings who all support one another. But, of course, there are those beings in heaven and on Earth that fall behind, either wittingly or unwittingly and become laggard beings who fall out of the Divine Plan by working against it. They attempt to slow down and retard the forward growth of spiritual evolution. The Fall from Paradise is not a myth, fairy tale, or metaphor.

Every moment of our lives we are given the same choice as Adam and Eve in the Garden of Eden or Lucifer before the throne of God. Do we align our personal spiritual evolution with the Divine Plan, or do I rebel against the true, beautiful, and good? Do I make the courageous effort to climb the mountain of spirit to the summit of my higher self? The choice is ours as a human to become an Angel or fall back into animality as a demon or unconscious nature-spirit. The path is not easy, but the rewards are divine.

Michaelic Verse
by Rudolf Steiner

We must eradicate from the soul all fear and terror of

what comes toward us out of the future.

We must acquire serenity in all feelings and sensations about the future.

We must look forward with absolute equanimity to all that may come,

and we must think only that whatever comes is given to us

by a world direction full of wisdom.

This is what we have to learn in our times.

To live out of pure trust in the ever-present help of the spiritual world.

Surely nothing else will do if our courage is not to fail us.

Let us properly discipline our will, and let us seek

the inner awakening every morning and every evening.

BIBLIOGRAPHY

- Andreæ, Johann Valentin. *Reipublicæ Christianopolitanæ descriptio*. Argentorati: Sumptibus hæredum Lazari Zetzneri, Strasbourg, 1619.

- Andreæ, Johann Valentin. *Johann Valentin Andreae's Christianopolis; an ideal state of the seventeenth century*. translated from the Latin of Johann Valentin Andreae with an historical introduction. by Felix Emil Held. The Graduate School of the University of Illinois, Urbana- Champaign, 1916.

- Arnold, Edwin Sir. *The Light of Asia, or The Great Renunciation (Mahâbhinishkramana): Being the Life and Teaching Gautama, Prince of India and Founder of Buddhism (As Told in Verse by an Indian Buddhist)*. Kegan Paul, Trench, Trübner & Co., London, 1879.

- Avari, Burjor. *India: The Ancient Past: A History of the Indian Sub-Continent*. Routledge, New Edition, 2007.

- Barnwell, John. *The Arcana of the Grail Angel: The Spiritual Science of the Holy Blood and of the Holy Grail*. Verticordia Press, Bloomfield Hills, 1999.

- Barnwell, John. *The Arcana of Light on the Path: The Star Wisdom of the Tarot and Light on the Path*. Verticordia Press, Bloomfield Hills, 1999.

- Blavatsky, H. P. (Helena Petrovna). *Isis Unveiled: A Master-Key to the Mysteries of Ancient and Modern Science and Theology*. J. W. Bouton. New York, 1878.

- Blavatsky, H. P. (Helena Petrovna). *The Key to Theosophy: Being a Clear Exposition, in the Form of Question and Answer, of the Ethics, Science and Philosophy for the Study of Which the Theosophical Society Has Been Founded*. The Theosophical Publishing Company, Ltd. London, 1889.

- Blavatsky, H. P. (Helena Petrovna). *The Secret Doctrine: The Synthesis of Science, Religion and Philosophy*. The Theosophical Publishing Company, Ltd. London, 1888.

- Blavatsky, H. P. (Helena Petrovna). *The Voice of Silence: Being Extracts from the Book of the Golden Precepts.* Theosophical University Press, 1992.

- Bockemuhl, Jochen. *Toward a Phenomenology of the Etheric World: Investigations into the Life of Nature and Man.* Anthroposophic Press, Spring Valley, N. Y., 1977.

- Campanella, Tommaso. *The City of the Sun.* The ProjectGutenberg Ebook, David Widger, 2013.

- Colum, Padriac. *Orpheus: Myths of the World.* Floris Books. Colum, Padriac. The Children's Homer. MacMillan Co., 1946.

- Colum, Padriac. *The Tales of Ancient Egypt.* Henry Walck Incorporated, New York,1968.

- Crawford, John Martin. *The Kalevala: The Epic Poem of Finland.* John B. Alden, New York, 1888.

- Gabriel, Douglas. *The Eternal Curriculum for Wisdom Children: Intuitive Learning and the Etheric Body.* Our Spirit, Northville, 2017.

- Gabriel, Tyla. *The Gospel of Sophia: The Biographies of the Divine Feminine Trinity,* Volume1. Our Spirit, Northville, 2014.

- Gabriel, Tyla. *The Gospel of Sophia: A Modern Path of Initiation,* Volume 2. Our Spirit, Northville, 2015.

- Gabriel, Tyla and Douglas. *The Gospel of Sophia: Sophia Christos Initiation,* Volume 3. Our Spirit, Northville, 2016.

- Gabriel, Douglas. *The Spirit of Childhood.* Trinosophia Press, Berkley, 1993.

- Gabriel, Douglas. *The Eternal Ethers: A Theory of Everything.* Our Spirit, Northville, 2018.

- Gabriel, Douglas. *Goddess Meditations.* Trinosophia Press, Berkley, 1994.

- Gebser, Jean. *The Ever Present Origin.* Ohio University Press, 1991.

- Green, Roger Lancelyn & Heather Copley. *Tales of Ancient Egypt.* Puffin Books, New York, 1980.

- Harrison, C. G. *The Transcendental Universe; Six Lectures on Occult Science, Theosophy, and the Catholic Faith.* George Redway, London 1893.

- Harrison, C. G. *The Transcendental Universe; Six Lectures on Occult Science, Theosophy, and the Catholic Faith.* Delivered Before the Berean Society, edited with an introduction by Christopher Bamford. Lindesfarne Press, Hudson, 1993.

- Hamilton, Edith. *Mythology.* Little Brown And Co., Boston, 1942.

- Harrer, Dorothy. *Chapters from Ancient History.* Waldorf Publications, Chatham, 2016.

- Hazeltine, Alice Isabel. *Hero Tales from Many Lands.* Abingdon Press, New York, 1961.

- Heidel, Alexander. *The Babylonian Genesis: The Story of Creation.* University of Chicago Press, Chicago, 1942.

- Hiebel, Frederick. *The Gospel of Hellas.* Anthroposophic Press, New York, 1949.

- Jocelyn, Beredene. *Citizens of the Cosmos: Life's Unfolding from Conception through Death to Rebirth.* Continuum, New York, 1981.

- König, Karl. *Earth and Man.* Bio-Dynamic Literature, Wyoming, Rhode Island, 1982.

- Kovacs, Charles. *Ancient Mythologies and History.* Resource Books, Scotland, 1991.

- Kovacs, Charles. *Greek Mythology and History.* Resource Books, Scotland, 1991.

- Landscheidt, Theodor. *Sun-Earth-Man a Mesh of Cosmic Oscillations: How Planets Regulate Solar Eruptions, Geomagnetic Storms, Conditions of Life, and Economic Cycles.* Urania Trust, London, 1989.

- Laszlo, Ervin and Kingsley, Dennis L. *Dawn of the Akashic Age: New Consciousness, Quantum Resonance, and the Future of the World.* Inner Traditions, Rochester Vermont, 2013

- Plato. *The Republic.* Dover Thrift Editions, 2000.

- Sister Nivedita (Margaret E. Noble) & Coomaraswamy, Ananda K.. *Myths of the Hindus and Buddhists*. Henry Holt, New York 1914.

- Steiner, Rudolf. *Ancient Myths: Their Meaning and Connection with Evolution*. Steiner Book Center, 1971.

- Steiner, Rudolf. *Christ and the Spiritual World: The Search for the Holy Grail*. Rudolf Steiner Press, London, 1963.

- Steiner, Rudolf. *Foundations of Esotericism*. Rudolf Steiner Press, London, 1983.

- Steiner, Rudolf. *Isis Mary Sophia: Her Mission and Ours*. Steiner Books, 2003.

- Steiner, Rudolf. *Man as a Being of Sense and Perception*. Steiner Book Center, Vancouver, 1981.

- Steiner, Rudolf. *Man as Symphony of the Creative Word*. Rudolf Steiner Publishing, London, 1978.

- Steiner, Rudolf. *Occult Science*. Anthroposophic Press, NY, 1972.

- Steiner, Rudolf. *Rosicrucian Esotericism*. Anthroposophic Press, NY, 1978.

- Steiner, Rudolf. *Rosicrucian Wisdom: An Introduction*. Rudolf Steiner Press, London, 2000. GA 425

- Steiner, Rudolf. *The Bridge between Universal Spirituality and the Physical Constitution of Man*. Anthroposophic Press, NY, 1958.

- Steiner, Rudolf. *The Evolution of Consciousness*. Rudolf Steiner Press, London, 1926.

- Steiner, Rudolf. *The Goddess from Natura to the Divine Sophia*. Sophia Books, 2001.

- Steiner, Rudolf. *The Holy Grail: from the Works of Rudolf Steiner*. Compiled by Steven Roboz. Steiner Book Center, North Vancouver, 1984.

- Steiner, Rudolf. *The Influence of Spiritual Beings Upon Man*. Anthroposophic Press, NY, 1971.

- Steiner, Rudolf. *The Reappearance of Christ in the Etheric*. Anthroposophic Press, NY, 1983.

- Steiner, Rudolf. *The Risen Christ and the Etheric Christ*. Rudolf Steiner Press, London, 1969.

- Steiner, Rudolf. *The Search for the New Isis the Divine Sophia*. Mercury Press, N.Y., 1983.

- Steiner, Rudolf. *The Spiritual Hierarchies and the Physical World*. Anthroposophic Press, N.Y., 1996.

- Steiner, Rudolf. *The Tree of Life and the Tree of Knowledge*. Mercury Press, NY, 2006.

- Steiner, Rudolf. *The True Nature of the Second Coming*. Rudolf Steiner Press, London, 1971.

- Steiner, Rudolf. *Theosophy*. Anthroposophic Press. New York, 1986.

- Steiner, Rudolf. *Wonders of the World, Ordeals of the Soul, Revelations of the Spirit*. Rudolf Steiner Press, London, 1963.

- Steiner, Rudolf. *World History in Light of Anthroposophy*. Rudolf Steiner Press, London, 1977.

- Tappan, Eva March. *The Story of the Greek People*. Houghton Mifflin Co., Boston 1908.

- van Bemmelen, D. J. *Zarathustra: The First Prophet of Christ*, 2 Vols. Uitgeverij Vrij Geestesleven, The Netherlands, 1968.

APPENDIX—
COSMOLOGICAL
CHARTS

Diagram 1
Elohim †
Incarnations of the Earth

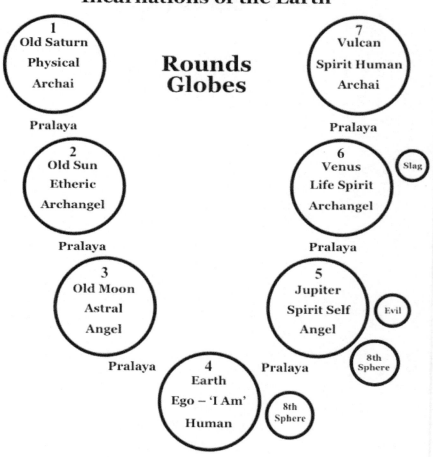

Rounds
Globes

1
Old Saturn
Physical
Archai

Pralaya

2
Old Sun
Etheric
Archangel

Pralaya

3
Old Moon
Astral
Angel

Pralaya

4
Earth
Ego – 'I Am'
Human

8th Sphere

7
Vulcan
Spirit Human
Archai

Pralaya

6
Venus
Life Spirit
Archangel

Slag

Pralaya

5
Jupiter
Spirit Self
Angel

Evil

8th Sphere

Pralaya

† Spirits of Form, Greek: Exousíai, ἐξουσίαι; Latin: Potestates; English: Powers, Authorities; Hebrew: Ělōhīm, אֱלֹהִים - plural of אֱלוֹהַ, Ělōah. "God(s), Heavenly Power(s)."

Diagram 2

7 Conditions of Consciousness

"Neither can they die any more: for they are equal unto the angels;
and are the children of God, being the children of the resurrection." Luke (20:36)

Old Saturn
Deep Trance
Consciousness
Upper
Devachan

Atman
Vulcan
Moral
Intuition
Universal
Consciousness

"Each condition of consciousness can only run its course in seven conditions of life; each condition of life in seven conditions of form. That is 7 x 7 x 7 conditions. In fact, an entire evolution such as that of the Earth passes through 7 x 7 x 7 conditions of form. Our Earth was once Saturn; this went through seven conditions of life and each condition of life through seven conditions of form, Therefore you have forty-nine conditions of form upon Saturn, forty-nine upon the Sun, forty-nine upon the Moon, etc.; 7 x 49 = 343 conditions of form. Man passes through 343 conditions of form in the course of his evolution." †

Old Sun
Dreamless Sleep
Consciousness
Lower
Devachan

Budhi
Venus
Moral
Inspiration
Hearing
Music of the
Spheres

"Jesus answered them,
Is it not written
in your law, I said,
Ye are gods?"
John (10:34)

Old Moon
Dream
Consciousness
Astral World

Manas
Jupiter
Moral
Imagination
Psychic or Soul
Consciousness

Earth
Waking
Consciousness

† Rudolf Steiner,
The Apocalypse of St. John,
Lecture X June 28th, 1908 (CW 104)

Diagram 3

7 Main Epochs of Earth Evolution

Polarian Epoch
Hyperborean Epoch
Lemurian Epoch
Atlantean Epoch
5th Post-Atlantean Epoch ←┐
6th Post-Atlantean Epoch
7th Post-Atlantean Epoch

7 Post-Atlantean Periods ↓

1st Post-Atlantean Period
Old Indian Period
2nd Post-Atlantean Period
Old Persian Period
3rd Post-Atlantean Period
Egypto-Chaldean Period
4th Post-Atlantean Period
Greco-Roman Period
5th Post-Atlantean Period
Anglo-Germanic Period
6th Post-Atlantean Period
Russian Period
7th Post-Atlantean Period
American Period

The 5th Post-Atlantean Epoch is divided into
7 Post-Atlantean Periods of 2,160 years

Diagram 4

7 Atlantean Periods (Sub-Races)

1st Rmoahals
2nd Tlavtlis
3rd Toltecs
4th Original Turanians
5th Ur Semites
6th Akkadians
7th Mongolians

7 Post-Atlantean Periods

1st Old Indian Period
1st Old Persian Period
3rd Egypto-Chaldean-Babylonian-Hebrew Period
4th Greco-Roman Period
5th Anglo-Germanic Period
6th Russian Period
7th American Period

'Today the idea of civilization has already superseded the idea of race'
Rudolf Steiner, Munich, May 8th, 1907

"To this [Atlantean] Root-Race belong the following Sub-Races:
Firstly the Rmoahals, secondly the Tlavtlis, thirdly the Toltecs,
fourthly the original Turanians, fifthly the original Semites,
sixthly the Akkadians, seventhly the Mongols. Still further back
we come to the continent of Lemuria, between Africa, Asia and
Australia." Rudolf Steiner, *The Foundations of Esotericism*
Lecture XXIV – Berlin, October 26th, 1905 (CW 93a)

Diagram 5

7 Post-Atlantean Periods

The Age of Cancer
Old Indian Period   ♋   **The Etheric Body**
                                           7,227 B.C.-5,067 B.C.

The Age of Gemini
Old Persian Period   ♊   **The Astral Body**
                                           5,067 B.C.-2,907 B.C.

The Age of Taurus
Egypto-Chaldean Period   ♉   **Sentient-Soul**
                                           2,907 B.C.-747 B.C.

The Age of Aries
Greco-Roman Period   ♈   **Intellectual-Soul**
                                           747 B.C.-1,414 A.D.

The Age of Pisces
Anglo-Germanic Period   ♓   **Consciousness-Soul**
                                           1,414 A.D.-3,574 A.D.

The Age of Aquarius
E. European Period   ♒   **Spirit-Self**
                                           3,574 A.D.-5,734 A.D.

The Age of Capricorn
American Period   ♑   **Life-Spirit**
                                           5,734 A.D.-7,894 A.D.

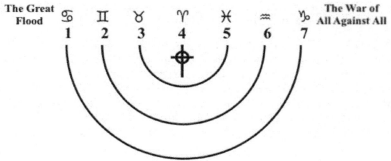

The Great Flood ♋ ♊ ♉ ♈ ♓ ♒ ♑ The War of All Against All
        1 2 3 4 5 6 7

Diagram 6

The Cosmic Year – Post-Atlantean Epochs

5th Post Atlantean Period   7,227 B.C.-7,894 A.D.

1. ♋ 2. ♊ 3. ♉ 4. ♈ 5. ♓ 6. ♒ 7. ♑

6th Post Atlantean Period   7,894 A.D.-23,014 A.D.

1. ♐ 2. ♏ 3. ♎ 4. ♍ 5. ♌ 6. ♋ 7. ♊

7th Post Atlantean Period   23,014 A.D.-38,134 A.D.

1. ♉ 2. ♈ 3. ♓ 4. ♒ 5. ♑ 6. ♐ 7. ♏

"What is important for us is the fact that the position of the Sun at the spring equinox moves backward, passing through the whole Zodiac little by little. It traverses the whole Zodiac until it finally returns to the original position, taking approximately 25,920 years. These 25,920 years are termed the Platonic Year, the Cosmic Year. The exact figure varies according to the various methods of calculation. However, we are not concerned with exact figures but with the rhythm this precession entails. You can imagine that a cosmic rhythm must lie in this movement which repeats itself every 25,920 years. We can say that these 25,920 years are very important for the life of the Sun, for during this time the life of the Sun passes through one unit, a proper unit. The next 25,920 years are then a repetition. We have a rhythm in which one unit measures 25,920 years....

"On average, a human being takes eighteen breaths a minute. Not all breaths are equal, for those in youth differ from those in old age, but the average is eighteen breaths a minute. Eighteen times a minute we rhythmically renew our life. Multiply this by 60 and you have 1,080 times an hour. Now multiply by 24, and the number of breaths in twenty-four hours comes to 25,920!"

"A year has 365¼ days and if we divide 25,920 by 365.25 the answer is: nearly 71. Let us say 71 years, which is the average life-span of the human being. The human being is free, however, and often lives much longer; but you know that the patriarchal life-span is given as 70 years. The span of a human life is 25,920 days, 25,920 great breaths, and so we have another cycle wonderfully depicting the macrocosm in the microcosm. We could say that by living for one day, taking 25,920 breaths, we depict the Platonic Cosmic Year, and by living for 71 years, waking up and going to sleep 25,920 times — a breathing on a larger scale — we once again depict the Platonic Year." Rudolf Steiner, Dornach 28th, January 1916

Diagram 7

Nine-Fold Constitution of the Human Being

1. *Old Saturn*
Thrones – Warmth Ether
Spirits of Will
Primal Physical Body as Warmth

Sphere of Planet Saturn
Mineral Kingdom
4th Stage of the Archai

....

2. *Old Sun*
Kyriotetes – Light Ether
Spirits of Wisdom
Primal Etheric Body as Light

Sphere of Planet Jupiter
Plant Kingdom
4th Stage of the Archangels

....

3. *Old Moon*
Dynamis – Sound Ether
Spirits of Motion
Primal Astral Body as Movement

Sphere of Planet Mars
Animal Kingdom
4th Stage of the Angels

....

4. *Earth*
Exusiai – Life Ether
Donate "I Am" – Ego

Human – Earth & Moon
Sentient-Soul
Intellectual-Soul
Consciousness-Soul

....

5. *Future Jupiter*
Heavenly Sound Ether
Angel Stage

Jupiter + Two Moons
Holy Spirit – Wisdom
Spirit-Self (Manas)

....

6. *Future Venus*
Heavenly Light Ether
Archangel Stage

Venus + One Moon
Son – Love
Life-Spirit (Budhi)

....

7. *Future Vulcan*
Heavenly Warmth Ether
Archai Stage

Vulcan – No Moon
Father – Will
Spirit-Human (Atman)

ABOUT
DR. RUDOLF STEINER

Rudolf Steiner was born on the 27th of February 1861 in Kraljevec in the former Kingdom of Hungary and now Croatia. He studied at the College of Technology in Vienna and obtained his doctorate at the University of Rostock with a dissertation on Theory of Knowledge which concluded with the sentence: "The most important problem of human thinking is this: to understand the human being as a free personality, whose very foundation is himself."

He exchanged views widely with the personalities involved in cultural life and arts of his time. However, unlike them, he experienced the spiritual realm as the other side of reality. He gained access through exploration of consciousness using the same method as the natural scientist uses for the visible world in his external research. This widened perspective enabled him to give significant impulses in many areas such as art, pedagogy, curative education, medicine, agriculture, architecture, economics, and social sciences, aiming towards the spiritual renewal of civilization.

He gave his movement the name of "Anthroposophy" (the wisdom of humanity) after separating from the German section of the Theosophical Society, where he had acted as a general secretary. He then founded the Anthroposophical Society in 1913 which formed its center with the construction of the First Goetheanum in Dornach, Switzerland. Rudolf Steiner died on 30th March 1925 in Dornach. His literary work is made up of numerous books, transcripts and approximately 6000 lectures which have for the most part been edited and published in the Complete Works Edition.

Steiner's basic books, which were previously a prerequisite to gaining access to his lectures, are: *Theosophy, The Philosophy of Freedom, How to Know Higher Worlds, Christianity as a Mystical Fact,* and *Occult Science.*

ABOUT THE AUTHOR, DR. DOUGLAS GABRIEL

Dr. Douglas Gabriel is a retired superintendent of schools and professor of education who has worked with schools and organizations throughout the world. He has authored many books ranging from teacher training manuals to philosophical/spiritual works on the nature of the divine feminine. He was a Waldorf class teacher and administrator at the Detroit Waldorf School and taught courses at Mercy College, the University of Detroit, and Wayne State University for decades. He then became the Headmaster of a Waldorf School in Hawaii and taught at the University of Hawaii, Hilo.

He was a leader in the development of charter schools in Michigan and helped found the first Waldorf School in the Detroit Public School system and the first charter Waldorf School in Michigan. Gabriel received his first degree in religious formation at the same time as an Associate's Degree in computer science in 1972. This odd mixture of technology and religion continued throughout his life. He was drafted into and served in the Army Security Agency (NSA) where he was a cryptologist and systems analyst in signal intelligence, earning him a degree in signal broadcasting. After military service, he entered the Catholic Church again as a Trappist monk and later as a Jesuit priest where he earned PhD's in philosophy and comparative religion, and a Doctor of Divinity.

As a Jesuit priest, he came to Detroit and earned a BA in anthroposophical studies and history and a MA in school administration. Gabriel left the priesthood and became a Waldorf class teacher and administrator in Detroit and later in Hilo, Hawaii. Douglas has been a sought-after lecturer and consultant to schools and businesses throughout the world and in 1982 he founded the Waldorf Educational Foundation that provides funding for the publication of educational books. He has raised a great deal of money for Waldorf schools and institutions that continue to develop the teachings of Dr. Rudolf Steiner. Douglas is now retired but continues to write a variety of books, including a novel and a science fiction thriller. He has four adult children who keep him busy and active and a wife who is always striving towards the spirit through creating an "art of life." She is the author of the *Gospel of Sophia* trilogy. These books and others are available at Ourspirit.com.

TRANSLATOR NOTE

The Rudolf Steiner quotes in this book can be found, in most cases, in their full-length and in context, through the Rudolf Steiner Archives by an Internet search of the references provided. We present the quoted selections of Steiner from a free rendered translation of the original while utilizing comparisons of numerous German to English translations that are available from a variety of publishers and other sources. In some cases, the quoted selections may be condensed and partially summarized using the same, or similar in meaning, words found in the original. Brackets are used to insert [from the author] clarifying details or anthroposophical nomenclature and spiritual scientific terms.

We chose to use GA (Gesamtausgabe—collected edition) numbers to reference Steiner's works instead of CW (Collected Works), which is often used in English editions. Some books in the series, *From the Works of Rudolf Steiner*, have consciously chosen to use a predominance of Steiner quotes to drive the presentation of the themes rather than personal remarks and commentary.

We feel that Steiner's descriptions should not be truncated but need to be translated into an easily read format for the English-speaking reader, especially for those new to Anthroposophy. We recommend that serious aspirants read the entire lecture, or chapter, from which the Steiner quotation was taken, because nothing can replace Steiner's original words or the mood in which they were delivered. The style of speaking and writing has changed dramatically over the last century and needs updating in style and presentation to translate into a useful tool for spiritual study in modern times. The series, *From the Works of Rudolf Steiner* intends to present numerous "study guides" for the beginning aspirant, and the initiate, in a format that helps support the spiritual scientific research of the reader.

Printed in Great Britain
by Amazon

49691568R00106